Twayne's United States Authors Series

Sylvia E. Bowman, *Editor*

INDIANA UNIVERSITY

Wallace Stegner

TUSAS 282

Wallace Stegner

WALLACE STEGNER

By FORREST G. ROBINSON and
MARGARET G. ROBINSON

TWAYNE PUBLISHERS

A DIVISION OF G. K. HALL & CO., BOSTON

Library of Congress Cataloging in Publication Data

Robinson, Forrest Glen, 1940-
  Wallace Stegner.

  (Twayne's United States authors series ; TUSAS 282)
  Bibliography: p. 175–184
  Includes index.
  1. Stegner, Wallace Earle, 1909-   2.   Authors,
American— 20th century—Biography. I.   Robinson,
Margaret G., joint author.
PS3537.T316Z9   813'.5'2 [B]   76-54313
ISBN 0-8057-7182-4

FOR
OUR PARENTS

Contents

About the Authors

Forrest G. Robinson completed his Ph.D. at Harvard University in 1968. With the aid of a Knox Memorial Fellowship, he spent a year in England completing a dissertation on Renaissance epistemology. After three years on the faculty of the Harvard English Department, he moved to the University of California at Santa Cruz, where he is presently an Associate Professor of Literature. His scholarly publications include an edition of Sir Philip Sidney's *An Apology for Poetry* (1970) and *The Shape of Things Known: Sidney's Apology in Its Philosophical Tradition* (1972). Currently he is engaged in two major undertakings: a biography of the eminent American personologist, Henry A. Murray, supported by a Guggenheim Fellowship in 1972–73; and the coediting of the first two volumes of the complete correspondence of Mark Twain.

Margaret G. Robinson took her bachelor's degree with honors in English literature at Radcliffe College in 1970 and her master's degree in library science at San Jose State University in 1973. She is presently employed as a reference librarian at the University Library, University of California at Santa Cruz. *Wallace Stegner* is her first major publication.

Preface

This first full-length book about Wallace Stegner will not be the last, for other critics will want to look more carefully at topics and problems which we have examined in brief. Nonetheless, in what follows we have turned our attention to what we consider the key elements in Stegner's development. Since much of his writing is autobiographical, and since the values that inform all of his work have deep roots in personal experience, Chapter 1 presents a detailed sketch of Stegner's life — especially of his youth and early adulthood. The uneasy union of Stegner's parents — strong, shiftless George and gentle Hilda — and the sharp contrast between Stegner's two boyhood homes — East End, Saskatchewan, a desolate prairie wheat town, and Salt Lake City, Utah, which represented sanctuary and the beginnings of culture — were seminal experiences. The series of dichotomies that they embodied — ignorance versus culture, individualism versus community, brute strength versus the law — pervade Stegner's writing from the beginning to the present and form his thematic center of gravity.

From the man, we turn to his work. Chapters 2 through 5 depart from absolute chronology and survey the Stegner canon in generic categories: historical nonfiction, short fiction, and the novels. History comes first because it makes explicit themes and values that take less direct expression in Stegner's fiction. Chapter 2 examines all but one of his full-length historical works, as well as a collection, *The Sound of Mountain Water* — the rich essence of his short nonfiction. Once again, a dichotomy dominates. As Stegner reviews the past of the arid intermountain West, he discovers two types of immigrants: the Mormons, who came to settle the land and husband its resources, and the Gentiles — like his own father — who "skimmed the cream" from the Land of Milk and Honey and left. However, Chapter 2 also introduces a third, more hopeful alternative; John Wesley Powell, Colorado River explorer, dedicated government scientist, and a small "d" democrat, provides an historical model of masculine responsibility for the heroes of Stegner's subsequent fictional works.

Chapter 3 begins with a brief survey of Stegner's critical writing. A Western realist with an almost constitutional aversion to "beautiful thinking," Stegner will not be long remembered for his criticism. The canon is short, unified, casual, and almost self-consciously "professional" in its point of view. Nevertheless, it presents and skillfully defends an intriguing critical hypothesis, the "personal heresy." According to Stegner, art is no more than the imposition of form upon personal experience: the central artistic problem, therefore, is the imposition of form "without loss of truth." The remainder of Chapter 3 deals with Stegner's short fiction in light of this standard. While many of his short stories are completely satisfying artifacts, we have chosen to view them primarily as a series of experiments which anticipate more important technical developments in his later and longer work. The short stories constitute a microcosm of Stegner's maturation as an artist — more precisely, of his developing mastery of the problem of point of view.

In Chapters 4 and 5 we turn to the novels. Necessarily, in this first full-scale treatment of Stegner, we have had to devote more than a little space to plot exposition, the identification of historical models for fictional places and persons, and clarification of the biographical circumstances surrounding the creation of each work. In the pages remaining, we have focused our attention upon the themes that dominate Stegner's fiction: initiation, maturity, identity, in short, growing up — reconciliation or resignation as the case may be. We have also chosen to concentrate on two major areas of technical development: the gradual mastery of point of view — especially of the first person narrator — and Stegner's steady progress toward what he has called "the middle ground."

"The middle ground" is a simple but crucial concept which we nave identified as the key to the understanding and judgment of Stegner's work. Briefly stated, the term refers to the dramatic rendering of historical persons, places, and events in a way that contributes to the discovery and articulation of continuities between past and present. Accordingly, "the middle ground" is more than a critical precept; it also implies a set of values. A culture-hungry boy from Saskatchewan, an historian and novelist, an American realist in the tradition of William Dean Howells, Wallace Stegner has been consistently preoccupied with the question of cultural continuities. Occasionally, this preoccupation has proved limiting. For example, in conjunction with strong personal prepossessions, it has resulted in an at times unbalanced view of the Mormons. In many of the best novels and short stories, however, prepossession becomes the point of view of a fictional narrator and thereby an artistic strength. Our overview of Stegner's fiction concludes with a detailed analysis of *Angle of Repose,* a melding of theme and technique that comes startlingly close to perfection, the novel of "the middle ground."

Stegner's most recent novel, *The Spectator Bird,* was published after the contours of this volume had reached their final form. Fortunately, we were able to read the novel in manuscript, and to reflect on its considerable merits. With Joe Allston (suffering from "a bad case of the sixties") as its narrator, *The Spectator Bird* can be viewed as a kind of sequel to *Angel of Repose.*

Irascible, uncertain, feeling obsolete and facing what he imagines to be his imminent death, Joe confronts hard, but for him, familiar questions: "How to respect myself when I know I'm confused and cowardly. How to respect a world where nothing I believe in is valued. How to live and grow old inside a head I'm contemptuous of, in a culture I despise." Such questions arise in a novel whose central theme — the search for meaning and personal identity in the past — will be equally familiar to Stegner's readers. As he reviews his life, Joe finds few continuities and therefore few consolations. His mother, a poor, struggling immigrant, died before he was mature enough to value her properly. Her memory induces guilt, as does the memory of Curtis, Joe's only child, whose aimless life and death were the result, Joe feels, of his failure as a parent. And Curtis' demise lends painful confirmation to his father's sense of discontinuity. It is in this dark mood that Joe undertakes what develops into the novel's main business — a review of his trip, in 1954, to Denmark in search of his mother's home and a link with his past.

In sifting through old records Joe reminds us, of course, of Lyman Ward. Joe and Lyman also share several personality traits — irascibility, skepticism, discontent, common sense — and an obsession with the past. Indeed, it is fair to say that more than a little of Lyman Ward has rubbed off on Joe Allston in the transition from *All the Little Live Things* to *The Spectator Bird.* This is not particularly surprising, especially in view of the fact that the novel that falls between them, Lyman's novel, *Angle of Repose,* is

Stegner's most fully integrated, most complex, most compelling and satisfying work. In this light, it is also not surprising that the frame structure of *Angle of Repose* has its counterpart in *The Spectator Bird*. Lyman, amidst the ruins of the present, ruminates in the past, mutters into his tape-recorder, and slowly, along links reluctantly acknowledged, comes back to himself. In reviewing the records of his trip to Denmark, Joe undergoes a similar process of self-discovery. In his case, however, the records are personal diaries, and he reads them aloud in nightly installments to his wife, Ruth. At the center of what unfolds is Joe's amorous brush with a fascinating and mysterious countess — a love affair barely avoided and at the time only dimly intuited by Ruth. Less central, but related, is the discovery that Joe's mother came to America not for freedom and the main chance, but for sanctuary. In both stories potential uprootedness and painful separation appear in high relief. In the record of his precarious but real fidelity to Ruth, however, Joe glimpses the antidote to disconnectedness, and the key to the human potential for creating continuities in history. "It has seemed to me that my commitments are often more important than my impulses or my pleasures, and that even when my pleasures or desires are the principal issue, there are choices to be made between better and worse, bad and better, good and good .... In every choice there is a component, sometimes a big component, of pain."

The Spectator Bird will be a splendid addition to Stegner's *oeuvre*. Although it is a slender volume, with less scope than its immediate fictional predecessor, it is in the legacy of *Angle of Repose* and therefore in Stegner's richest vein.

This book got its start in life when Page Stegner suggested that we undertake the TUSAS volume on his father. At that time, now, and in the several years between, we have been grateful for the opportunity. From the outset Wallace Stegner has been an ideal subject. Obviously, we have enjoyed his books. Moreover, we have had the benefit of his full cooperation. Interviews, a bibliography, articles not easily located, books out of print and inaccessible — all of these have been ours for the asking. He has given us detailed instructions for a trip through the heart of his favorite territory — a trip we plan to take. And we have sampled his wife Mary's wit and good cooking. If we express no more than gratitude here, consider it craven deference to convention.

Whatever virtues this volume may possess reflect back on the

Preface

widely acknowledged distinction of Wallace Stegner; the defects reflect on us alone. We have been saved from myriad errors and oversights by a host of generous friends and colleagues. To those who read and criticized the manuscript — Michael Cowan, Thomas Farber, James D. Houston, Dorothy and Paul Loughrey, Paul Skenazy, Judith E. Smith, John Solomon, and Kevin Starr — we are deeply grateful. We benefited from timely advice on politics from David Thomas, on history from John Dizikes, and on labor from William Friedland. Henry A. Murray, an inspiration in all things, introduced us to his own version of Louis Pasteur's utterance, "chance and the prepared mind." Elaine Tringali, one among several pillars of skill and patience in the College V Faculty Service Center, typed the entire manuscript. More recently, we are grateful for the assistance of the Crown College Faculty Service Center. And Annette Gordon, mother and mother-in-law, prepared the index. At their leisure and in peace, may they all read shelves of Stegner.

FORREST G. ROBINSON
MARGARET G. ROBINSON

Chronology

1909   Wallace Stegner born February 18 in Lake Mills, Iowa, the second son of George and Hilda Paulson Stegner.

1914   Family moves to East End, Saskatchewan.

1921   Family moves to Salt Lake City, Utah.

1925–
1930   Stegner attends the University of Utah. Freshman English with Vardis Fisher stimulates a growing interest in creative writing.

1930   Enters the graduate English program at the University of Iowa.

1933   Leaves college to nurse his mother through a fatal bout with cancer.

1934   Reenrolls at Iowa. Marries a fellow graduate student, Mary Stuart Page. Takes a first teaching job at Augustana College, a small denominational school in Rock Island, Illinois.

1935   Moves to a post at the University of Utah. Completes his doctoral degree with a dissertation on Clarence Earl Dutton, literary naturalist.

1937   Son Page born January 31. Stegner's first major fictional effort, *Remembering Laughter,* wins the Little, Brown novelette prize. Accepts position at the University of Wisconsin. Begins work on *The Big Rock Candy Mountain,* his great family novel.

1938   *The Potter's House.*

1939   Joins the staff of the Breadloaf writers' conference. Meets Robert Frost and Bernard DeVoto. Buys a home in Greensboro, Vermont.

1940   *On a Darkling Plain.* Invited to teach in the Harvard creative writing program. Moves to Cambridge. Deepens his friendship with DeVoto and other adversaries of contemporary literary Marxism. George Stegner commits suicide.

1941   *Fire and Ice.*

1942   *Mormon Country.*

1943   *The Big Rock Candy Mountain.*

1944   Stegner becomes embroiled in the bitter literary quarrel between DeVoto and Sinclair Lewis. Leaves Harvard to help *Look* magazine research a wartime series on racial and religious intolerance.

1945   *One Nation.* Stegner accepts a professorship at Stanford University. Moves to Los Altos Hills, California.

1947   *Second Growth.*

1950   *The Preacher and the Slave* and *The Women on the Wall.* Takes an around-the-world tour sponsored by the Rockefeller Foundation.

1951   *The Writer in America.*

1953   Makes a return trip to East End, Saskatchewan.

1954   *Beyond the Hundredth Meridian.* Travels to Norway in search of family roots.

1956   *The City of the Living.*

1961   *A Shooting Star.*

1962   *Wolf Willow.*

1964   *The Gathering of Zion.*

1967   *All the Little Live Things.*

1969   *The Sound of Mountain Water.*

1971   *Angle of Repose* is published and wins the Pulitzer prize. Stegner retires after twenty-six years of service to the Stanford creative writing program.

1974   *The Uneasy Chair.*

1976   *The Spectator Bird.*

CHAPTER 1

The Life

I *Local Habitations*

OPEN your atlas to the largest map of the United States. Be sure the map is detailed enough to include such small towns as Lake Mills, Iowa, and international enough to make room for that narrow corridor of southern Canada that borders the United States east and west between Washington and Minnesota, north and south between the 49th and 50th parallels. Lake Mills may elude you. It lies about ten miles — a fraction of an inch on your map — below the Minnesota border on a line running almost due north from Des Moines. Now, with Lake Mills as your point of departure, draw an imaginary line, more north than west, across Minnesota. You will pass near Blue Earth, New Ulm, Willmar, Alexandria, and Pelican Rapids before you reach the state border. A jot to your left and you will be in Grand Forks, North Dakota. From there start a new line, now more west than north, through Rugby and Kenmare, North Dakota, and on across the 49th parallel into southwestern Saskatchewan. Bring this second line to a halt at the western edge of a sharp dip in the Frenchman River. Your map may not show it, but that point is no more than a hairbreadth from the site of East End. A third line, moving in almost equal measure south and west, will bring your eye to Great Falls, Montana. A fourth, dropping due south, comes to rest at Salt Lake City. Now trace your way east through northern Colorado and central Nebraska to Iowa City, Iowa. It remains to join Iowa City to Lake Mills and the figure is complete. The somewhat unlovely hexagon which results encloses what we may think of as Wallace Stegner country.

More precisely, the six points which define the hexagon are the places where Stegner grew up, where the human stuff of his writing unfolded itself. Between these very specific loci are the regions that inform his people: rich farmland on the east; the semiarid plains in

17

the center; to the west, the monumental Rockies giving way to a waste of sand and salt that Brigham Young chose to make fertile. On top is a slender triangle of Saskatchewan and East End, the smallest and most important town of all. It is Stegner's Hannibal, and the Frenchman River is his Mississippi. "I remember that town in Saskatchewan with great clarity," he once remarked. "If every writer is born to write one thing, that [town] was my thing."[1]

We have jumped ahead, however, for Wallace Stegner entered his country farther east, at Lake Mills, Iowa, on February 18, 1909. Home for his mother and father, for his older brother Cecil, and soon for young Wallace, was Grand Forks, North Dakota. But his birth occurred during a visit to the farm of his maternal grandfather, Chris Paulson. Memories are dim here,[2] especially of grandmother Paulson, who died young of overwork and possibly of tuberculosis. The daughter of a prosperous burgher of Ulvik, Norway, she left her idyllic home at the head of Hardangerfjord for the United States, and ultimately for Iowa, in about 1880. Grandfather Paulson, from the same Norwegian town, was less wellborn but stronger, and so better remembered. He appears pretty much as his grandson, Wallace Stegner, remembers him in Nels Norgaard, the stern, silent, self-righteous quantum of aging vitality who figures prominently in the opening pages of *The Big Rock Candy Mountain*. His vigor took different forms. Most visibly it was a thicket of coarse white hair that refused to lie down. It was also a walk on his hands to the barn when he was sixty years old.[3] Finally, it was the decision to remarry when he was about forty-five. Admirable vigor, yes, but the light of his eye fell on his daughter Hilda's close friend. It happened in about 1905, and it happens again in *The Big Rock Candy Mountain,* a novel which Stegner has characterized as "family history reasonably straight." Hilda Paulson could not abide such vigor. She expressed her disapproval by abandoning Lake Mills for Grand Forks, North Dakota, where she went to work for a relative. Like Elsa Norgaard, the fictionalized Hilda of *The Big Rock Candy Mountain,* she left home and security and what was intolerable in her father for an unknown town and an uncertain future.

Enter George Stegner, the model for Bo Mason in his son Wallace's fictionalized recounting of the family history. Young, rangy, athletic, irresponsible, a gambler and therefore something of a fighter, resourceful, musical in a primitive sort of way, basically a drifter, he had a knack for getting into trouble and a more useful knack for landing on his feet — usually. His background is vague, but his earliest American forebears were a pair of Bavarian brothers who settled in Pennsylvania during the 1820s. George's father, a branch of the second generation, fought in the Civil War, was wounded, and may have spent some time in the Andersonville prison. The details of his later life and rather early death are either forgotten or too painful to remember. His wife, George's mother, survives in grandson Wallace's memory as an incontinent old woman who went crazy "and had to be taken away by a Mountie to the Provincial asylum because she took to standing silently in the door of the room where my brother and I slept — just hovered there for heaven knows how long before someone discovered her watching and listening in the dark."[4] The rest is as obscure as that hallway.

What drew Hilda Paulson to George Stegner is equally unclear. *The Big Rock Candy Mountain* portrays young George as a romantic figure, a strapping, robust, good-natured rascal. It may be that Hilda saw him that way. But what did she think of his "blind pig"? Of his hotel with its clientele of transients, local wasters, and garrulous drunks? Of his penchant for taking life as a series of gambles? What did she make of his violence, his shady friends, his marginal morals? In short, how did an instinctively pious, naive, peace-loving farm girl from somewhere in Iowa get involved with a slick roughneck in Grand Forks, North Dakota? Although an answer is not easily come by, George's good looks and his ready smile must have been part of it. But the real key may lie in the striking difference between Chris Paulson and George Stegner. In bitter flight from what she must have viewed as unnatural and hypocritical in her father, it is not altogether improbable that Hilda should have been irresistibly drawn to what seemed natural and spontaneous in George.

Whatever the explanation, George and Hilda were soon married and the parents of two sons. Apparently horizons were pretty low in Grand Forks; the family had departed before young Wallace's memory flickered into existence. In fact, his first recollections are situated outside of the Stegner country; he retains vague memories of a spell in Bellingham, Washington, followed by a move south to Redmond, where they lived in a tent and ran a lunchroom for loggers. The first really clear image is a prophetic one, for it focuses on a precocious storyteller: "I can remember sitting on some boarding house steps in Seattle when I was there telling some neighbor kid that I was half Indian and half Jew, but don't tell anybody! I don't know where I got that!" Presently the boardinghouse becomes a kind of orphanage, a wretched place where the oatmeal was so vile that its memory still prompts indigestion. The children's "home" was a necessary expedient: it gave Hilda time to work and time to keep herself and the boys alive. She left them there only until she discovered how terrible the conditions really were. Meanwhile George had disappeared, and memory is not clear about where he had gone. Perhaps he was looking for new opportunities in Alaska or in the Peace River country of Alberta. Nor is it clear how mother and children survived in Seattle, or how long they stayed. Finally Hilda swallowed her pride and returned home to security and a cool reception in Lake Mills. It cannot have been a happy time for her.

For young Wallace, less sensitive to the implications of separation and less vulnerable to the friction in his grandfather's house, the months before the outbreak of World War I were warm and relatively secure. "I remember my step-grandmother and my mother and the other women sitting around reading the paper and clucking their tongues in that peculiar Norwegian woman's fashion, sighing on an indrawn breath — eeeh! I was crawling around under the clothes horse in rainy weather with the smell of drying laundry all around me, listening to the women's conversation. I was too young to have been in school. I would have been just five."

II *Whitemud*

Hilda was in a bind. On the one hand, she had good reasons for staying in Lake Mills; for, however cool the reception, and however emotionally complex the circumstances, it was home. There were familiar sights and sounds, old friends, the feeling of permanence, security for her children. All of this she felt drawn to, and all of this George was unable or had failed to provide. On the other hand, there was her father. And there was his wife who, in ceasing to be a close friend, had certainly not become her mother. Their hospitality seems to have been tentative, begrudging, the kind of charity that springs from a desire to humiliate. Finally, and most important, there was George, whom Hilda loved almost in spite of her hunger for stability, and who, in the spring of 1914, was sending her halting letters from a place called East End. End of what? she must have wondered. Lake Mills was small, but who had even heard of East End? And Canada! Still, the letters probably had the charm that George could muster when he wanted something. Moreover, the letters made promises about a fresh start in a new town; about free land; about work done and money saved; and about the building of a house. If he actually wrote about a house—and most probably he did—then that was the promise that got Hilda out of Iowa and out of her bind. Late that spring she bundled her boys onto a train headed for Saskatchewan. As the station faded to a speck at the end of the track, she must have been as resolute as Elsa Mason was when she left home for the last time: "She knew that she would stick to Bo now no matter what came. She had made her bed, and this time she would lie in it."[5]

For the next six years, until he was almost twelve, Wallace Stegner lived in and around East End. In later life he would distinguish himself as a novelist of places. This place, of all the places in Stegner country, was the one that formed him most decisively, that bruised him into an awareness of himself and his special identity, and that loaded his memory with the landscapes and faces and voices and events that appear in much of his best writing. Whitemud—his fictional name for East End—must have been in his mind when he said, "I don't believe you can write about anything ... without drawing deeply on your own experience."[6] Happily enough for his biographer, Stegner has written copiously and intimately about East End. A major section of *The Big Rock Candy Mountain* takes the town as its setting and the barely fictionalized events of Stegner's youth as its substance. *Wolf Willow*, which mingles history and fiction with personal reflection, focuses on East End and includes long passages of explicitly autobiographical narrative. Given Stegner's testimony to the importance of these years, and given the degree to which they dominate his work, it is altogether appropriate that we dwell with them at some length, and that we do so as much as possible in his own voice.

The last leg of the journey from Lake Mills to East End involved a stagecoach, a lot of dust, and Buck Murphy, "a red-faced cowpuncher with a painful deference to ladies and a great affection for little children." Stegner remembers riding "the sixty miles on Buck Murphy's lap, half anesthetized by his whiskey breath," and confounding both "mother and Murphy by fishing from under his coat a six-shooter half as big as I was."[7] At the end of the jolting ride was another frontier type, one as romantic as the sodden cowpuncher and probably easier to abide at close quarters — a Mountie! "Holstered at his belt he had a revolver with a white lanyard, and he was altogether so gorgeous that I don't even remember meeting my father"(101). But whatever happy illusions the cowboy, the guns, and the law engendered in the head of her son, Hilda Stegner must have been experiencing a more complex mixture of emotions as they rolled into East End.

On the bright side was the reunion with George and being a family again. That much she would have approved. But what he had said was a town looked distressingly like a construction camp. The Mountie's red coat was the only bright color in the picture. Rather than houses and stores, the eye fell on a rutted road, over-turned equipment, piles of lumber, yellow mud. Lying at the east end of the Cypress Hills, the town was situated in the lowland along the Frenchman River. On three sides — north, south, and west — the benches rose several hundred feet above the rooftops, providing sanctuary. Eastward, the plains spread away, perfectly, tediously flat. There were no trees to speak of. Construction trains were in evidence, but it would be a year or so before rail connections with the outside world were complete. And what of the house George had promised? He kept his promise, only later; for now home was a derailed dining car.

But there was some money, and George had found work. Memories are vague about what he was doing. Perhaps he owned some of that equipment and was contracting it out. Maybe he had a boardinghouse. Maybe both. At any rate, he had money and work; that much was good. Better yet, a closer look indicated that there was a semblance of a town. Here and there among the derailed train cars and shacks one could make out a general store, a frame hotel, the boardinghouse that George may have run. The Village Council, representing one hundred and seventeen souls, had met for the first time at the end of March, 1914. By June — about the time of the family reunion — the local newspaper was in operation; July brought the first annual stampede; in August, England (and Canada with her) entered into war against Germany; September saw the first signs of winter, and it saw them with the aid of the new street lights. It was not all bad in East End. Even if the boys came home with lice in their hair; even if the place was filthy and "bare as a picked bone"; even if they had to spend their first winter in a two-room improvised shack, they were together, and things were getting better fast. Hilda would stick.

Wallace Stegner's memories of the years in East End take two rather different forms. First there are patterns, not so much distinct images as large remembered rhythms of season and landscape. These are supplemented by sharper pictures of the family and friends, of animals, and of events whose memory rekindles the full range of emotions they first gave life to. The rhythms recreate setting and mood while the specific images add life, human meaning, and a reassuring fixity in remembered space and time.

The biggest thing in Sasketchewan is the sky. Next in size, and much bigger in the life of a boy, is the land. Depending on the context in which he remembers it, Wallace Stegner's reminiscences on the site of his boyhood vary about as much as the land remains monotonously the same. In one mood, "By most estimates, including most of the estimates of memory, Saskatchewan can be a pretty depressing country" (5). In another, "There was never a country that in its good moments was more beautiful" (8). But these are adult reflections. At other moments, we get closer to the feel of a boy's land with a boy's river running through it. "What I remember are low bars overgrown with wild roses, cutbank bends, secret paths through the willows, fords across the shallows, swallows in the clay banks, days of indolence and adventure where space was as flexible as the mind's cunning and where time did not exist. That was at the heart of it, the sunken and sanctuary river valley. Out around, stretching in all directions from the benches to become coextensive with the disk of the world, went the uninterrupted prairie" (6).

If the land and sky were constants, they were constants only in their conformity to the annual round of seasonal change. Saskatchewan weather is a cycle of extremes. Winter comes in like a wolf. Almost overnight the air begins to bite at ears and toes; life moves indoors; tempers get shorter with the days and with close quarters. The land seems flatter than ever, numb and tired. Then comes the snow, a mixed blessing of color and cold and winter sports and slush and more cold. From time to time there are blizzards, some so violent that men get lost in the middle of the street and freeze to death a few yards from safety. Less frequent are the Chinooks, warm winds that raise the temperature fifty degrees in an hour and stir brief presentiments of spring. But the warmth is as fleeting as the illusions it gives rise to. A day or so later the land and sky are locked in gray ice that may not loosen until late April.

Just about the time that East Enders have given up on it, spring arrives. What had seemed irrevocably dead is suddenly just as irrepressibly alive. The snow disappears, the river breaks up under the sun, splashes of color spread along the cutbanks, in the brush, and in the cheeks of children gone slightly mad with space and freedom and the great outdoors. May and June witness temperate weather, mild days interspersed with welcome rain showers. Sometimes the rain persists in thunderstorms during July and August; sometimes the wind is fresh and cool and exhilarating, "a thing you tighten into as a trout tightens into fast water" (7). More often, under a pittance of rain, the land dries; the wind is heavy and sullen; the atmosphere is oppressive. When there is no wind at all, the days seem long and downright unbearable. Waves of heat put a crazy, exotic rippling on the horizon. The sky is an enormous blue dome. Dust devils materialize and vanish in an instant. On the worst days boys play in the river while their parents look forward to the cooler weather ahead.

Seasonal patterns bore with them the steady rhythm of human activity. For Wallace Stegner the fall of 1914 meant school. That first year the class gathered in a room above Bill Anderson's pool hall. The next year the students went through their paces in a shack next to the butcher shop on Main Street. Finally, in about 1916, the town provided its young scholars with a brick schoolhouse. It was here that an earnest teacher "tried, inadequately and hopelessly, to make a European" (24) of Wallace Stegner. However badly the chronicles of a civilized past and remote continents served the practical realities of an unwashed frontier, school set the mind in motion, and it was a place to shine. While his older brother excelled in sports, Wallace lost himself in books and the praise that comes to good boys who read them. "Our house contained some novels of George Barr McCutcheon and Gene Stratton-Porter, a set of Shakespeare in marbled bindings with red leather spines and corners, and a massive set of Ridpath's *History of the World*. I handled them all, and I suppose read in them some, uncomprehendingly, from the time I was five'' (27).

What George Stegner did during the winter is not clear in his son's memory. Weather permitting, he must have worked on the gabled white frame house that he had promised Hilda. They moved in during the second year. When the war sent prices up, he rented some sandy bottom land and grew acres of potatoes. Wallace remembers being let out of school to gather them into sacks and drag them to the hotel to be stored. Another year George was out during October and November shooting ducks to freeze for the winter. But if Wallace's memory is at all accurate, his father spent most of his time hanging around waiting for the odd job and playing poker. Gambling was at the center of his life, taking chances on potatoes and ducks and cards.

And wheat. During the summer, when school was out, the landscape and the activities changed. Fifty miles south of East End, smack on the Montana border, was a half section — three hundred and twenty acres — of flat prairie land that George Stegner planned to cultivate. Why he selected remote acreage right in the middle of ''Palliser's Triangle'' — an area that early surveyors judged to be unarable semidesert — is a mystery; for better land was available closer to town. Perhaps the international boundary tempted him; perhaps he had more than wheat in mind. In any case, he was not alone in his willingness to gamble a lot of hot work on just enough rain at just the right time. If you won, you won big. With just fifty acres producing twenty bushels each and with the price of wheat at three dollars a bushel you could come home with a handsome profit. Imagine what you could do with half a section.

But it all hung on the rain. The first summer George worked the land, 1915, he took the two boys with him and left Hilda in town. They plowed, planted, and then built a shack while they waited for the rain — which came in the right quantities and at about the right time. Nothing spectacular, but when the threshers and binders had been paid in September there was plenty left to take back to East End. The rhythm of the five following summers was pretty much the same — plow, plant, wait. Once the shack was completed, Hilda came with them. She tried to coddle trees and plants into some kind of permanence. But it was futile. Each June, the ground was as bare as the day she first arrived.

During the long vigil between sowing and reaping, Wallace and his brother Cecil busied themselves with killing the gophers that menaced the wheat. The numbers of their victims were no more impressive than the chilling ruthlessness of their methods: "We lived an idyl of miniature savagery, small humans against rodents. Experts in dispensing death, we knew to the slightest kick and reflex the gophers' way of dying: knew how the eyes popped out blue as marbles when we clubbed a trapped gopher with a stake, knew how a gopher shot in the behind just as he dove into his hole would sometimes back right out again with ridiculous promptness and die in the open, knew how an unburied carcass would begin within a few hours to seethe with little black scavenger bugs, and how a big orange carrion beetle working in one could all but roll it over with the energy of his greed, and how after a few days of scavengers and sun a gas-bloated gopher had shrunk to a flattened wisp of fur" (275–76). Here, then, was another of Saskatchewan's patterns: brutal violence and death on a large scale. To Wallace Stegner's chagrin as an adult, the young Wallace fell in all too well with the harsh homestead code; during at least one summer, he and Cecil collected more gopher tails than anyone else in the area — and received a prize for their accomplishment.

Land, sky, seasons, school, homestead, violence, death — these are all but one of the grand patterns and movements that lodged themselves in Wallace Stegner's memory. It remains to speak of disaster and its inevitable offspring, frustration. With the possible exception of the first year, disaster was as steady in the pulse of the Saskatchewan years as wind and sky. It took a greater variety of shapes and it was much harder to predict, but it came in almost every year between 1915 and 1920, and it seemed to get worse. Some of the disasters were minor and brought an element of excitement with them. In Stegner's words, there was the night "we came out into the hard cold from the Pastime Theater and heard the firehouse bell going and saw the volunteer fire department already on the run, and followed them up the ditch toward the glow of the fire, wondering whose house, until we got close and it was ours" (17). For months after, it was a good game to imagine faces and scenes in the ceiling where the chemicals left a stain. Or take "the fifty-one below, eighty-mile-an-hour blizzard of 1916, which marooned teachers and children in the schoolhouse for a day and a night and part of the next day before my father and others could beat their way in on a long string of lariats and lead us home along that lifeline with our stocking caps pulled down over our faces and our hands up the sleeves of our mackinaws'' (262). That was exciting too. The same might be said for the flood of 1917. But it was much less exciting when the hotel burned down and took with it all the potatoes that George had so prudently harvested. There was nothing very festive about Christmas that year: "dinner was bacon and potatoes and canned-saskatoon pie, and my brother and I fell silent and ashamed when on Christmas morning other kids came around to show off their presents'' (261). George's duck hunting, equally prudent, was equally frustrating: the birds rotted during an unseasonable warm spell.

All of this trouble could have been borne with relative ease had the summer wheat continued to flourish. But the mild success of 1915 was the prologue to five seasons of total failure. In 1916 the crop rotted under too much water. From 1917 on, there were four years of drought. You could get by if you harvested every other year. You could survive, barely, if you hit it every third year and your credit was good. But five years running without a crop was disaster pure and simple.

Finally, and most destructive of all, there was the flu epidemic which swept across the continent and reached East End late in 1918. On Halloween night, just two weeks before the end of World War I, the first victim was hauled into town on a buckboard. From that point on, it was gauze masks and eucalyptus oil and the schoolhouse full of the sick and dying; it was confusion, inadequate supplies, aching joints; and it was unforgettable. The chronicle of the flu epidemic appears in *The Big Rock Candy Mountain, On a Darkling Plain, Wolf Willow,* and in numerous stories and articles. All of the Stegners were deathly sick, particularly George, but all survived. Others were less fortunate. Whole families were wiped out in the space of a few agonizing days. Sixty or more — about ten percent of the town — were in their graves before it was over. That disaster imprinted itself on Wallace Stegner's memory like a scar.

So far we have surveyed East End as if from a distance. From that rather remote vantage it looks about as barren and uncivilized and blighted a place as one could imagine. While such an impression is probably fairly accurate, it overlooks the people and events that fill out the vivid foreground of boyhood memories. We have neglected Mah Li and Mah Jim, the Chinese brothers who befriended Wallace, and whose trust he betrayed the night he helped overturn their outhouse. And P.K., who got trapped in a cave behind the Stegner house and had to be revived by artificial respiration. The omnipresent animals, both pets and victims: Caesar, the family mutt; the four prime ermine and the mink that Wallace and Cecil trapped near a dam on the river; the incurably crippled colt who wore iron leg braces, and whose pathetic but necessary death was a bitter lesson in life. Characters: the fabulous Tattooed Man who appeared like an exotic amphibian in the Frenchman River; "the albino traveling salesman who sported among us and palpitated girlish hearts for a day" (295); wild, unhappy Irene, who got drunk, took off her clothes, and chased Wallace down the street; best of all, Reno Dodds, so skinny he was known as Slivers, but the best bronco-buster East End ever saw. There were pranks, like raiding T.B.'s shack, stealing his enormous "forty-four" and some dynamite caps, and then trying to burn it all down "just for the hell of it" (293). And close calls: the time Wallace put a "twenty-two" short through his big toe; and an unforgettable bellyflopper from over thirty feet. Like bright colored leaves, the memories — more than we can mention here — drift through the mind. Such was the woof and warp of youth in frontier Saskatchewan, the stitching that seamed the days and weeks and years into a memorable whole.

It may be that East End was, as Wallace Stegner has written, "as good a place to be a boy . . . as one could well imagine" (306). But, if it was good, it was also hard, tough, and uncompromising. Wallace in *Wolf Willow,* like Bruce in *The Big Rock Candy Mountain,* was small for his age, somewhat withdrawn, ambitious for approval and yet ambivalent about the harsh code that was its price. He did well in school, but the rewards came from his teachers and Hilda, not from his peers. He was self-consciously a runt in a community that valued size, where "the strong bullied the weak, and the weak did their best to persuade their persecutors, by feats of courage or endurance or by picking on someone still weaker, that they were tough and strong" (129). We wonder how good it was to suffer the humiliation of shameful inadequacies that Wallace describes: "As for me, I was a crybaby. My circulation was poor and my hands always got blue and white in the cold. I always had a runny nose" (130). How much happiness did it take to generate the reflection, "I grew up hating my weakness and despising my cowardice and trying to pretend that neither existed" (131)? Memory may have played him false when it told Wallace Stegner that a boy's life in East End was all that good.

In fact the East End years can be understood best in terms of dichotomies. Some of them were probably evident enough to the boy who experienced them, while others were merely implicit. Stegner himself gives us our cue: "The 49th parallel ran directly through my childhood, dividing me in two" (81). But what the 49th parallel divided in Stegner's early life was not two nations — nations, after all, which are in many ways similar. We do best to view the border not geographically as an imaginary line that separates one place from another, but symbolically as a chasm that stretches between two totally incompatible attitudes toward life. On one side is East End, without culture, without traditions, violent, barren, beautiful in its primitive way, but the product of a hard code. On the other side is Salt Lake City, Stegner's next real home, where the Mormons had brought water to a barren land and made it productive. They forged culture, fostered traditions, created their own unique sense of community, valued gentleness, and found peace. Most simply, Salt Lake was civilized while East End was not.

The cultural chasm separating East End and Salt Lake City had its human counterpart in the differences between George and Hilda Stegner. They were the key dichotomy. We have already opened, and left open, the problem of how they came together in the first place. It remains to touch briefly on what their differences meant to their son during his youth, and how they reappear in his art. Stegner again gives us our cue, this time through his self-projection in *The Big Rock Candy Mountain:* "If a man could understand himself and his own family, Bruce thought, he'd have a good start toward understanding everything he'd ever need to know."[8] Bruce goes on to describe his father as "a self-centered and dominating egoist who insists on submission from his family and yet at the same time is completely dependent on his wife, who is in all the enduring ways stronger than he is."[9]

The frustrations that George Stegner encountered in Saskatchewan, and later in Salt Lake and Reno, did little to nourish what was potentially good-natured in him and everything to intensify what was irascible and violent. Young Wallace's father was a figure of terror who might, at any moment, lash out in contempt for "mama's boy," or who might rush at him with irrational violence. For a time father's brutality had its designed impact: "Be-

cause I was what I was, and because the town went by the code it
went by, I was never quite out of sight of self-contempt or the contempt of my father or Alfie Carpenter or some other whose right to
contempt I had to grant'' (132). But, along with the humiliation,
there are memory traces of the hostility and resentment that grew as
hot in him as the sting in the seat of his pants after a fierce licking:
"After that licking I lay out behind the chopping block all one
afternoon watching my big dark heavy father as he worked at one
thing and another, and all the time I lay there I kept aiming an
empty cartridge case at him and dreaming murder" (16).

If Wallace's father was the concrete embodiment of all that was
harsh and uncivilized about the frontier, then just as surely his
mother was the synthesis of all that was potentially gentle and
civilized in life. George "went strictly by the code," but Hilda "had
sympathy for anyone's weakness except her own" (130). A sanctuary from the hostile world, she advocated education, music,
respectability, probity, and resisted the semibarbarous masculinity
that East End and her husband tried to impose upon her children.
Usually she succeeded, particularly with Wallace; and she succeeded more and more as time and experience impressed her son
with the brutish inadequacies of his father's ways. Her support and
loving protection may have meant the shame of being "mama's
boy," but they were also the indispensable first promptings toward
the culture and discipline that were to be Wallace Stegner's portion
in life.

Memories of mother and father have faded over the years. Quite
naturally they are at their brightest and sharpest in *The Big Rock
Candy Mountain,* where the differences between Bo and Elsa,
George and Hilda, are so consistently portrayed that they form a
major theme. But with Bo Mason out of his system, Wallace Stegner was free to turn to the positive ideal of masculinity that was his
father's opposite — the gentle, civilized, and civilizing man who is
a recurring figure in his work. John Wesley Powell — the explorer
of thc Grand Canyon, thc planner for the West, and the subject of
Stegner's *Beyond the Hundredth Meridian* — is the quintessence of
the type. From his mother, he acquired a model of feminine excellence that required few if any modifications. She is Elsa Mason,
and she reappears, with important modifications, in several more
recent Stegner heroines. Her claims on memory and affection have
not diminished.

Though the East End years were only the first chapters in his life, they were also the years that Wallace Stegner would return to first and most often in later life. Moreover, the dichotomies that colored his boyhood and flooded his memory — the hard code versus the gentle code, civilization versus barbarism, individual versus community, all compressed in father and mother — became the center of thematic gravity in all of his writing. When the family left East End in 1920 Wallace was not yet twelve; but the principal characters and major issues of his fiction were already part of his experience.

III   *Chance and the Prepared Mind*

George's reasons for leaving East End are obvious: disaster and frustration. But his motives for moving the family to Great Falls, Montana, the fourth point on our map of the Stegner country, are obscure. Bo Mason moves to Montana in order to capitalize on an unwatched border, fast cars, and plenty of Canadian liquor; and George may have had the same things in mind. Whatever Wallace's father's reasons, the fifteen months in Great Falls were a revelation to the young boy; for the town was much bigger than East End, and therefore so was his world. In Great Falls, Wallace saw his first lawn and got his first job mowing one. And the Missouri River must have made the Frenchman seem like a puddle. Situated at the gateway to the Rocky Mountains, Great Falls is one of a closely spaced series of falls that held up Lewis and Clark on their journey west. For Wallace and Cecil, however, the river created no obstacles. For the best part of two summers, it was a playground of swimming holes and river islands where they enjoyed "a very Huckleberry Finnish kind of experience." When they were not in school or working, the neighborhood children spent a lot of time stealing crab apples from local orchards. Word had it that irate farmers lurked behind trees with shotguns and just enough rock salt to put a sting in the behinds of young felons. But the guns never went off, and the apples were awfully good — as good as life itself for a twelve-year-old boy just in from the barren frontier.

But George Stegner was not the settling kind. During the months in Great Falls, the family lived in two houses. During the following decade in Salt Lake, they lived in something like twelve more. After a few months in a house George would begin to get itchy. A few weeks more and the scratching began. "Come on, Hilda," he would say, "let's get out of this place before the roof caves in on us." There was no point in resisting. The move to Salt Lake in midsummer, 1921, was an example of George's scratching.

The itch that set it off was gambling; or, more precisely, speculation in mines and grain futures. Salt Lake was an ampler terrain; it provided more operating room. After all, the Jazz Age was in full swing, even in provincial Utah. With a little money and with a lot more luck, a man could get ahead. Apparently George had enough of both to prosper during the next ten years, for most of his dozen or so houses were fairly substantial.

Salt Lake in 1921 was a community defined by its own unique dichotomy — a dichotomy which may help to explain why the Stegners stayed there as long as they did. On one side there was the order and permanence of the dominant Mormon culture with its emphasis on group solidarity, whether in the family, church, or community. These were the qualities in the city that appealed to Hilda and that molded her younger son's values. Later on both of them would think of Salt Lake as home — or as being, at least, as close to home as they could come. On the other side were the Gentiles, a minority distinguishable from the Mormons in several crucial ways. Obviously, there were religious differences; but more important perhaps, was the Gentile's individualism, his relative indifference to groups of any kind, his gravitation to private opportunities in business, and his tendency to abandon things and places when they ceased to satisfy his personal expectations. This element in Salt Lake attracted George; it was also this Gentile ethos that tempted his older son.

Our dichotomy is, of course, too simple, too absolute. As Wallace Stegner would be the first to insist, it fails to make room for Mormon individualists and for Gentiles who value groups; but such an admission would not be a rejection of the general truth that the dichotomy lays open. That general truth is very much in evidence in *Mormon Country,* one of Stegner's numerous tributes to his Utah home. In general, he argues, the Mormons were all that their Gentile neighbors were not: "They were as indefatigable, obedient, stalwart, and united a people as the world ever saw. Their record in the intermountain region is a record of group living, completely at variance with the normal history of the West. The American Dream as historians define it did not fit these whiskered zealots. Theirs was a group dream, not an individual one; a dream of Millennium, not of quick fortune."[10] The chasm that yawned between the Mormons and the Gentiles was the same one that separated George and Hilda. But at least in Salt Lake there was something for both of them and for both of their sons.

The Utah years, about fifteen of them in all, were years of rapid and manifold growth for Wallace Stegner. Thanks to a couple of skipped grades, by the time he was sixteen he had finished high school. By now it was pretty clear that he liked books; he devoured them in lots of five or six gathered home each week from the local Carnegie library. At first he consumed whole shelves of adventure books written by the likes of G.A. Henty and H.M. Tomlinson. James Fenimore Cooper was another early favorite, along with Mark Twain. Then, during the summer of 1923, the family moved into a house that contained, among other things, a yard or so of Joseph Conrad's books. That was a decisive coincidence, for Conrad was to be a formidable model.

Writing also began to surface as a vocation. Much to his initial surprise, Wallace discovered that yarns about a boy's life on the frontier were exciting to his classmates in high school. In subsequent years he took spot assignments covering sports events for the Salt Lake *Tribune*. Tennis was a personal favorite, along with basketball. Fortunately, and perhaps as a symptom of general personal development, the East End "runt" grew eight inches during his fifteenth year.

But a taste for adventure books and a ready pen did not lead immediately to the decision to become a writer. In September, 1925, the tallish sixteen-year-old freshman who entered the University of Utah was more interested in his job and in girls than he was in career decisions. The job involved selling rugs and linoleum in the family business of a close friend and tennis partner. Steady money led to romance, girl friends, and midnight dashes to Saltair or the canyons in the rumble seat of a friend's souped up car. When it came at all, school work came in the early hours of the morning, squeezed in between dates and the store.

But if his college education lacked rigor, it nonetheless helped him to form important personal goals. By a happy accident Stegner's instructor in freshman English was Vardis Fisher, a budding novelist. Fisher's approval and encouragement led to further courses in advanced writing. Minor literary successes at the university and occasional writing for the *Tribune* were beginning to point Stegner in a fairly definite direction — definite enough, at any rate, to steer him clear of graduate work in psychology. When the chairman of that department offered him a fellowship, Wallace rejected the offer in favor of a more attractive proposition from the University of Iowa — financial aid toward a higher degree in English. In the fall of 1930, with literature in mind, Wallace left for Iowa City, the last junction in the Stegner country.

Meanwhile, the family had not been idle. Late in 1926, George and Hilda moved to Los Angeles, apparently pursuing some new scheme. Wallace decided to follow them and to enroll as a sophomore at the University of California at Los Angeles. He arrived in Los Angeles hemorrhaging from a recent tonsillectomy. Once recovered, he grew bored, decided to enter a local tennis tournament, drew young Ellsworth Vines in the first round, and was decisively trounced. Clearly there was little to hold him in such a lonely, unprofitable place as Los Angeles. He packed and returned to Salt Lake — home.

His parents returned in 1928. By that time Wallace had sacrificed a year of school to the rug and linoleum business while his boss was making the European tour. Cecil was working at one of the smelters and trying to get himself in shape for the major leagues by playing semiprofessional baseball. A successful career as a high school pitcher had been followed by marriage when he was seventeen. The marriage failed to work — that much was clear to the whole family. But there was baseball, the brightest thing in his brief life. In 1930, when he was twenty-three, Cecil was suddenly very sick with pneumonia and was almost as suddenly dead. Hilda mourned quietly while George exploded in violent, impotent grief.

At about the time that Cecil died, Hilda discovered that she had severe medical problems of her own. Her symptoms were diagnosed as cancer. The surgery that followed seemed to be successful, at least for the time being; not until the summer of 1931 did the dreaded symptoms begin to reappear. Wallace returned from a successful first year of graduate school to meet his mother in Salt Lake. She came in from Reno, Nevada, where George and a couple of other men were running a gambling casino, the Northern Club. As a gesture of pride, she presented her only remaining son with a secondhand Model A Ford. Together with one of Wallace's girl friends they drove down to Reno to survey father's latest speculation.

The contrasts that summer must have been painful. On one side there was George, aging, paunchy, dressed like a dude, submerged in a vulgar gambling operation. On the other side was Hilda, making light of regular x-ray treatments, trying to disguise the terrible pain that grew worse as the disease spread, looking silently and in vain for consolations that George either would not or could not provide. By the following June, when Wallace returned from a second year in Iowa City, the pain could no longer be concealed. George decided that a change of scene might help, so they drove south through Yosemite and then circled east to the family cabin on Fish Lake in southern Utah. It was there that it became agonizingly clear that Hilda had neither the strength nor the will to live much longer.

Her slow, appalling decline is described at length in *The Big Rock Candy Mountain*. In the fall of 1932, George and Hilda moved back to Los Angeles. In order to be within a day's drive of his mother, Wallace enrolled in the English graduate program at Berkeley. By the spring of the following year, Hilda's condition had so deteriorated that he decided to discontinue his studies and join his parents at Fish Lake. Soon the pain became so unbearable and death so imminent that Hilda asked to be moved home to Salt Lake. There, after more suffering than we care to recount, she died.

After the funeral father and son saw little of each other. When, seven years later, Wallace got word that his father had committed suicide in a run-down Salt Lake hotel, he must have shuddered with the recognition that such a dismal ending had been almost inevitable, not only in George's life, but also in the great family novel that he was writing. His parents, both in their lives and in their deaths, were the concrete symbols of two utterly antagonistic versions of the American Dream. Though neither dream came true — Hilda never got her permanent home, and her husband never struck it rich — it is certainly fair to say that George was the heavier loser. His desperate decline and suicide represented to his son the heartsick acknowledgment that there is "no Big Rock Candy Mountain, no lemonade springs, no cigarette trees, no little streams of alcohol, no handout bushes. Nothing. The end, the empty end, nothing to move toward because nothing was there."[11]

When Wallace Stegner left the University of Iowa in June, 1932, he had already completed his master's thesis, a cluster of short stories. With the support of his friend and teacher, Norman Foerster, he might have gone on to a doctorate in creative writing. Instead he decided, probably wisely, that teaching opportunities would be more abundant if he took a doctorate in English literature. He had a few credits from Iowa toward that degree when he entered the program at the University of California the following fall. But family problems and the fact that the Berkeley department demanded more philology than he could bear brought him to the conclusion that Iowa was where he belonged. Accordingly, he re-enrolled at Iowa for the spring semester of 1934.

Suddenly what had seemed simple became pleasantly complex. Upon arrival in Iowa City, Stegner discovered that there was a job open at Augustana, a private Lutheran college in Rock Island, Illinois. An additional but even more pleasant complication was Mary Page, a graduate student at Iowa, who by September of the same year was his wife. With the Great Depression in the back of his mind, and Mary in the front, Stegner accepted the job along with the weekly commute from Rock Island to Iowa City.

The next few months must have been a little mad. Augustana College was in the throes of a power struggle between the resident fundamentalists and a caucus of upstart evangelicals. Naturally, newcomers were the objects of suspicious scrutiny from both sides. Before long rumors began to spread that Stegner was at best an agnostic, at worst — perish the thought — an atheist, and out of sympathy with the principles of Christian education. Fortunately, during the summer of 1934 the University of Utah offered him a teaching post for the next academic year. Assured that Mormons were more tolerant of the heathen than his employers in Illinois, he seized the opportunity to return to Salt Lake. By the following summer, he had more than a year's teaching experience and his doctoral degree.

Stegner's doctoral dissertation was the product of another of those cycles of happy coincidence that steered him toward the career that was finally his. It all began during his junior year at the University of Utah when he was forced to miss a final examination in geology. His professor suggested that, as an alternative to the final, he compose an essay on Clarence Edward Dutton's masterpieces, *The Geology of the High Plateaus of Utah* (1880) and *The Tertiary History of the Grand Canyon District* (1882). The topic was a natural for a student who had adopted Utah as his home and whose parents owned a cabin in the plateau country at Fish Lake. The paper sparked an interest that was later rekindled by Norman Foerster at the University of Iowa. Foerster, who had written extensively about nature in American belles lettres, but who had neglected literary naturalists like Dutton, encouraged Stegner to fill in the gap. The upshot was the dissertation, "Clarence Edward Dutton: Geologist and Man of Letters," which was revised and published as *Clarence Edward Dutton: An Appraisal* by the University of Utah in 1936. Though not of great consequence in itself, the slim volume was a milestone on the road that led Stegner to John Wesley Powell, Bernard DeVoto, and the history of the American West.

During Wallace's first year or so at the University of Utah, he was absorbed in teaching and had little time for writing. There was the revision of his dissertation and the composition of two or three short stories — one of which, "Bugle Song," turned out to be the first installment on *The Big Rock Candy Mountain* — but for the most part his attention was divided between his students and his wife, who was expecting a child. In the fall of 1936, Stegner received an announcement that Little, Brown was sponsoring a novelette contest with twenty-five hundred dollars as the first prize. Drawing on the skeleton of a story from Mary's family closet, he completed and submitted a manuscript inside of eight weeks. When Little, Brown responded with a request for a photograph of the author, Stegner replied that he had a boil and asked if they could not do without the picture. When the response was negative, the picture was sent. Before long a victory telegram and a check for twenty-five hundred dollars arrived. When *Remembering Laughter* was published a few months after the birth of Page, a boy, on January 31, 1937, Wallace Stegner had a family and a first novel that one reviewer found "startlingly close to perfection."[12] From here on his vocation would be clear, his course fixed.

IV *The Career*

The Little, Brown prize, combined with almost two thousand dollars more for the *Redbook* publication of *Remembering Laughter,* brought a measure of confidence and financial security. Confidence prompted Stegner to visit the chairman of the English department with the suggestion that he be given tenure. The chairman congratulated him on his new book but counseled patience. A meeting with the president drew a similar response. Financial security now became an issue. In the spring of 1937, Stegner ran out of patience with the University of Utah and quit. He planned to take Mary and Page to the Virgin Islands where he would establish himself as a writer. What finally developed was far less romantic than a remote island hideaway but far more prudent. Leaving the baby in the good care of Mary's parents, the Stegners made a summer bicycle tour through England and France. They returned to the United States just in time for Wallace to accept a job teaching freshman English at the University of Wisconsin.

Madison was home for the next two years. For the first prolonged period in his life Stegner was living outside of the country that we have characterized as peculiarly his own. He could not have known it at the time, but he was out of the Stegner country for good. Physically, at any rate. By the end of the year, while living in a pleasant house on the shore of Lake Monona, Wallace began to work in earnest on *The Big Rock Candy Mountain*. Almost six years later, in 1943, it was finally completed. During the interim he published several short stories; a novella, *The Potter's House* (1938); two short novels, *On a Darkling Plain* (1940) and *Fire and Ice* (1941); and a tribute to the saints, *Mormon Country* (1942). Most of this writing, and certainly most of the best of it, takes its source in personal experience and its place in the Stegner country. In mind and in spirit, Wallace never left the familiar territory of his youth.

The following summer found the Stegners even farther from home, in New England. While Mary and Page stayed with friends in Vermont, Wallace spent a month at Yaddo, the artists' workshop in upstate New York. The session at Yaddo was not yet over when there was a phone call from Theodore Morrison, the director of the annual Breadloaf writers' conference just over the border in Vermont. A member of the staff had become ill, and someone was needed to fill in; Wilbur Schramm, Stegner's Iowa City roommate who had been teaching at the English School, had suggested Wallace as a replacement. Would he like to join them? It was Chance and the prepared mind again. For a young writer Breadloaf was literary Mecca, the gathering place for many of the most distinguished writers and publishers in the country. It was at Breadloaf, over a stretch of several summers, that Stegner enjoyed the company and friendship of Robert Frost, Bernard DeVoto, Theodore Morrison, and many others. It was a splendid opportunity, and he made the most of it. Before returning to Madison in September he purchased a farm that Mary had found in Greensboro, Vermont. They would be back.

The chance to get back came almost at once. Promotions were no more plentiful at Wisconsin than they had been at Utah. Just as Wallace's impatience began to smolder again, there was another phone call from Morrison who, during the academic year, was the director of the English A writing program at Harvard. It was Morrison's very good idea to staff the program with active writers, and it happened that a slot had fallen vacant. Again the door had opened, and again Stegner stepped through. During the next academic year, the Stegners lived in Newtonville, a suburb of Boston. Subsequent winters found them in a Cambridge apartment vacated by Henry Nash Smith. Wallace taught halftime in English A and gave the rest of his energy to writing. Among their close friends they numbered Frost, the DeVotos, and the Howard Mumford Joneses.

It was an exciting time to be in Cambridge. As the depression dragged on, and as the conflict that finally ended it took shape in Europe, political dispute grew more passionate. On the Left were the literary Marxists, led by F.O. Matthiesson. In what he viewed as the center — he considered himself a small "d" democrat — was DeVoto. With intellectual gunpowder manufactured in a seminar given by his friend, L.J. Henderson, DeVoto took shots at Marxists, system builders, and aesthetes. He took issue with the New Deal, rejected the dole, and joined Frost in venerating the sturdy Vermont yeoman who got by on hard work and three hundred dollars a year. Stegner's political opinions were not as firm as DeVoto's, but he was by nature suspicious of system builders whose minds, he felt, were closed like a trap. For a time, he joined the leftist Harvard Teacher's Union, but withdrew after the signing of the nonaggression pact between Russia and Germany.

As subsequent developments made clear, DeVoto had set his sights on bigger game than the local literary radicals. Like Stegner, he was from Utah; as a child he had rejected two dogmas, Mormonism and Catholicism. By the time he reached Cambridge as a Harvard undergraduate he had had his fill of systems. But if Harvard educated him, it did not make an Easterner of DeVoto.

Regional pride, resentment at the fact that Easterners took little notice of the West, resistance to a style that struck him as effete, and genuine love for rural New England — all of these elements were present in DeVoto's esteem for Vermont farmers and in his very vocal antagonism to "beautiful thinkers." Stegner understood his friend's position, and in some less extreme form he shared it. But it was not his intention to get entangled in the quarrel.

The entanglement started when DeVoto came to Stegner for some information on John Wesley Powell. DeVoto was preparing the Patton Lectures, later delivered at Indiana University in 1943 and published as *The Literary Fallacy* in 1944. His main thesis was simple and explosive. Most of the literary giants of the 1920s and 1930s had, out of ignorance and arrogance, totally misrepresented the times they lived in and wrote about. Too quick to condemn the country as a drab, materialistic wasteland, and too ready to propose foreign — especially Soviet — alternatives, such writers had neglected altogether the excitement, diversity, boldness, and native justice of the American people. Powell, on the other hand, was a writer who knew the country and its human potential like the back of his hand. As a scientist he proceeded not from abstractions and "beautiful" thoughts but from a firm grasp of American fact. He was the genuine literary hero; the others were fools and liars. DeVoto made grateful acknowledgment of Stegner's assistance in the preface.

A week before the publication of *The Literary Fallacy,* a section of the final chapter appeared as the feature article in *The Saturday Review of Literature.* The following week the same magazine issued a reply by Sinclair Lewis entitled "Fools, Liars, and Mr. DeVoto." Whatever the inadequacies of DeVoto's argument — and they were manifold — Lewis wasted little time with them; instead, he went straight for the man. Perhaps the most insulting moment in an insulting essay is Lewis' recollection of his first meeting with DeVoto: "I had never heard of him but I was interested in that frog-like face, those bright eyes, that boyish and febrile longing to be noticed. I was reasonably polite to him, and he was grateful. I saw him several times afterward, but his screaming, his bumptiousness, his conviction that he was a combination of Walter Winchell and Erasmus, grew hard to take, and it is a long time now since I have seen him."[13] The prose roars along in disorganized, brutal, almost unmitigated vilification. About midway, however, the storm subsides for a moment when Lewis pauses to take note of Stegner's part in the hateful book. Why DeVoto required Stegner's assistance in "that task, which any child with the extensive account of Powell in the 'Dictionary of American Biography' before him could do in ten minutes, is a puzzle. For Wallace Stegner, author of 'On a Darkling Plain,' 'The Big Rock Candy Mountain,' *et al.,* is already one of the most important novelists in America, an incomparably better writer than DeVoto, and a number of us go daily to the cathedral and pray that he will get out of Harvard, get away from all the cultural quacks like Mr. DeVoto, go back to Utah and Iowa, and put on the mantle of greatness that is awaiting him."[14]

If Lewis was trying to drive a wedge between DeVoto and Stegner, he failed. But how could Lewis have known that Stegner did not consider historians "cultural quacks"? How could Lewis have appreciated the fact that Stegner placed more value on Powell's contributions to American civilization than he did on most of the writers Lewis was defending? Little did Lewis realize that "one of the most important novelists in America" had it in mind to abandon the palace of art for a while in order to write Powell's biography. Lewis could not see that Stegner was in sympathy with the general substance of DeVoto's position, however much he might have regretted its tone. Stegner was less vocal about it than DeVoto, but he shared his friend's characteristically "Western" impatience with what he considered mannered, arrogant, and utopian in certain "Eastern" habits of mind. To their elegant Emerson he would reply with plain Mark Twain.

When Stegner finally left Cambridge, it was not to go in search of a "mantle of greatness." In March, 1944, Paul Buck, acting as provost in the absence of President James B. Conant, decided to release his overworked Harvard faculty a couple of months early. By that time Stegner had already arranged a leave of absence for the following year in order to work on an interesting and financially attractive project suggested by the editors of *Look* magazine. As part of the war effort, *Look* wanted to run a series of articles about racial and religious intolerance. Their eye fell on Stegner because he had recently completed some articles on anti-Semitism in Boston. And the timing was perfect. After a brief vacation in Mexico the Stegners moved to Martha's Vineyard. While Mary recuperated from a recent illness and looked after Page, Wallace submerged himself in the sociology of race relations.

That fall, with the articles on the East and South completed, and with just enough gasoline stamps for the trip, the Stegners drove West. Their journey took them to Montecito, California, where they took up quarters in a guest house on the estate of Mrs. Gardner Hammond. After the New Year, leaving Page with his grandparents, Wallace and Mary moved to New York where the final articles were completed in about three months. By that time the war was winding down, and the *Look* editors decided to cancel the series. Instead, in partial conformity with the original plan, the articles were published in a single volume, *One Nation,* later in the year. Exhausted, probably a little disappointed, the family reassembled at Montecito for a few months of sunshine and relaxation.

While Wallace golfed, napped, and took the air, Chance was preparing to open another door. Edith Mirrielees, an old friend from Breadloaf, had retired from her post as the principal teacher of creative writing at Stanford University. Stegner was offered a full professorship as her replacement. Saving Harvard the awkwardness of finding him expendable, he accepted on the condition that he could teach halftime. That summer the Stegners moved to Palo Alto. For the first time they had a permanent job and a permanent home.

To his delight, Stegner found the students at Stanford the most exciting he had yet encountered. Eugene Burdick was one of the first and best. Like many others, he was an ex-GI, four or five years older than ordinary students, experienced, enthusiastic, and in a hurry to get somewhere. Before long the writing program began to expand. Richard Foster Jones, the department head and an eminent scholar of literature, helped Stegner persuade his wealthy brother to lend his financial support. An initial gift of seventy-five thousand dollars made it possible to create fellowships for a master's program which combined rather rigorous course requirements with a creative thesis. Over time, thanks to Jones' brother's continued generosity, the endowment went well beyond half a million dollars, and the program flourished.

The offspring of Stegner's Breadloaf experience, the Stanford program added the professional discipline of a staff of working writers to the freedom and security of campus life. Staff members did not "teach" writing; rather, respecting the quality of the Fellows, they simply tried to create an atmosphere congenial to the creative process. A quick glance through *Twenty Years of Stanford*

Stories illustrates the continuing success of their efforts. Now nearing the end of its third decade, the Stanford Creative Writing Program remains a yeasty amalgam of Greenwich Village and Grub Street. It is the ultimate rebuff to those who contemn the "academic" artist, as well as tangible proof of the vitality of Wallace Stegner's original conception. When he resigned from Stanford in 1971, he left the program in the capable hands of Richard Scowcroft.

Sinclair Lewis was right about one thing: *The Big Rock Candy Mountain* did establish Wallace Stegner as a major American novelist. And if Lewis' admonition to seek fame in the West was not instrumental in Stegner's decision to move to California, it was at least inadvertently prophetic. The East End years were the most essential and possibly the most exciting; they were the raw experience from which Stegner's early writing took life. Salt Lake provided room for growth, a Western identity, and a hopeful pattern of personal and social alternatives. New England brought the exhilaration of first successes, initiation into the literary world, a model of rural civilization, and the emergence of refined regional perspectives. California, while outside the boundaries of the Stegner country, was close enough to seem like home. And it was the place where it was finally possible, after thirty-six years of almost constant motion, to put down roots.

The pattern of life for the Stegners during their nearly thirty years in the Stanford community has been comparatively stable. During the academic year the main activity has been teaching, more and more of it in later years. Especially in the last two decades, summers have found them in Greensboro, Vermont, their second home. There have been a few long trips, most notably an around-the-world lecture tour in 1950; journeys into the family past — Saskatchewan in 1953, Norway in 1954 — which finally resulted in *Wolf Willow;* and a sojourn in 1950 as writer in residence at the American Academy in Rome. There have also been occasional forays into the political arena. Long before ecology became fashionable, the Western experience made the Stegners active conservationists. During the Kennedy administration, Wallace served as assistant to the Secretary of the Interior (1961) — a post in which he helped to develop the National Parks Bill — and as a member of the National Parks Advisory Board (1962). But, more than anything else, the years since 1945 have been years of writing while at home in the foothills outside of Palo Alto.

In the course of three decades, Wallace Stegner has been enormously productive. In addition to hundreds of articles and short stories, he has written six major novels: *Second Growth* (1947), *The Preacher and the Slave* (1950), *A Shooting Star* (1961), *All the Little Live Things* (1967), *Angle of Repose* (1971), and *The Spectator Bird* (1976). He has also published two collections of short fiction, *The Women on the Wall* (1950) and *The City of the Living* (1956); two biographies, *Beyond the Hundredth Meridian: John Wesley Powell and the Second Opening of the West* (1954) and *The Uneasy Chair* (1974); a collection of critical essays, *The Writer in America* (1952); a historical monograph, *The Gathering of Zion: The Story of the Mormon Trail* (1954); and two volumes of essays and personal reflection, *Wolf Willow: A History, a Story, and a Memory of the Last Plains Frontier* (1964) and *The Sound of Mountain Water* (1969). Moreover, the depth of the Stegner canon has been as impressive as its breadth. In the past four decades, the American literary establishment, both academic and commercial, has accorded Wallace Stegner ample tribute. He has been elected to the American Academy of Arts and Sciences and to the National Academy of Arts and Letters. He has been awarded fellowships by such distinguished institutions as Phi Beta Kappa, the Huntington Library, the Center for Advanced Studies in the Behavioral Sciences, and the Guggenheim, Rockefeller, and Wenner-Gren Foundations. Finally, he has received a host of honors, including the Little, Brown novelette prize (1937), the O. Henry memorial award (1942, 1948, 1950), the Anisfield-Wolfe and Houghton Mifflin Life-in-America awards (1945), the Commonwealth Club gold medal (1968), and the Pulitzer prize for fiction (1971). In all, it has been stable, productive, distinguished, and civilized — very much as Hilda would have wished it.

CHAPTER 2

The Nonfiction

I *Clio and Calliope*

T HE dichotomies and tensions that we have observed in Wallace
Stegner's life are — to be perfectly bald about it — the key to
his work. We have taken note of this interplay between life and
work in *The Big Rock Candy Mountain* and in *Wolf Willow,* and
we will have occasion to see it again and again as we continue.
Stegner's nonfiction is no exception to this general rule. Indeed,
one justification for this chapter lies in the fact that the dichotomies we have found in the life take their clearest and most straightforward expression in the nonfiction.

The large majority of Stegner's nonfiction has to do with the
West, that region which lies beyond the hundredth meridian. But
we can be more specific. If we cut the cake as Stegner does, we will
divide the West into four subregions. There is the Northwest —
Oregon and Washington — about which he has little to say. There
is the Southwest, and again he is more or less silent. California is a
third subregion of the West, though at times Stegner's impulse is to
treat it — at least in its more recent history — as a cultural extension of the East. He is quite vocal about California. What remains
is Stegner country somewhat modified — Montana, Wyoming,
Colorado, Utah, Idaho, and Nevada — the Rocky Mountain West.
This is the area he knows best, and that he returns to most often.

Stegner approaches the Rocky Mountain West from a number of
different but closely related points of view. He comes as its product, the son of George and Hilda. As we have observed, his mother
and father are the key paradigm, the polarized models from which
other dichotomies spring. Historically and generally speaking, the
white man's West has been a rootless, violent place, characterized
by individualism and vulnerable to exploitation. In the same his-

torical and general terms, the woman's West has been the site of frustrated yearnings for permanence and stability, a place where traditions grow all too slowly, and where the absence of cooperation and community have been painful facts of life. In the most general terms, then, Stegner views the principal dichotomies in the past and present West as variations on the conflict between the values and actions of men and women. Given this general pattern, we will do well to remember that certain Western men have adopted the values of stability and cooperation and have acted upon them. In deviating from the normal pattern, they do not make themselves any the less men; but they are exceptions, and Stegner views such exceptions in a very positive light.

For the purposes of organization, we can divide Stegner's nonfiction into essays and books. Most of the latter we will discuss in subsequent divisions of this chapter. *One Nation* (1945) we will ignore altogether, and for several reasons. It was written with the editors of *Look* magazine and is therefore far from "pure" Stegner. Its most striking contents are pictures, and we are interested in words. Finally, though its words were enlightened and progressive in the last year of World War II, they have become dated in the intervening decades of social and political change. Of the more than one hundred and twenty-five essays we can touch only a few. Since many of the best essays have been preparations for books, we will encounter them in a more polished condition at one remove. Others will turn up in our discussion of the novels. The dozens of pieces that fall outside our focus are duly noticed in the bibliography appended to the end of this volume. For present purposes, we can turn to *The Sound of Mountain Water* (1969), a collection of Stegner's best, most representative essays. Written over a period of more than twenty years, these are the rich essence of his short nonfiction.

The Sound of Mountain Water is at once an historical reflection, a personal memory, and a study of the ways of remembering. To put it another way, the volume includes sections on history, on personal experience, and on methods of recording the cultural and personal past. Stegner gives fair warning when he acknowledges that the essays "were written over a period of more than twenty years," and that they reflect "no systematic approach and develop no coherent thesis."[1] Not surprisingly, the book is somewhat disconnected; at times adjacent sections seem forced rather than molded together; some of the essays, isolated from the contexts in which they originally appeared, include minor obscurities. But that is the price exacted in most collections of this kind. And with *The Sound of Mountain Water* the cost is slight while the rewards are substantial. However imperfect the stitching, the parts are uniformly impressive. Moreover, there are a few unifying threads. A steadily alternating current of acceptance and rejection, affection and scorn, runs between the covers. Like an inconstant mistress, the West propels her admirers through cycles of optimism and despair. And there are recurrent, and therefore unifying, acts of memory.

Historical memories arise first. They spring from the thought of water — or, rather, its scarcity — beyond the hundredth meridian: "The history of the West until recently has been a history of the importation of humid-land habits (and carelessnesses) into a dry land that will not tolerate them" (19). Aridity has been, and remains, the West's fatal unity. In its earliest stages, the frontier seemed almost infinite in its natural resources. But well before 1900 it was clear that buffalo, beaver, and gold were as finite as life itself. Indifference to drastically limited water supplies could have, and ultimately did have, even graver human and ecological consequences. Stegner learned this first as a boy in Saskatchewan. Later on, at about the time of the Dust Bowl, when parched Nebraska soil fell on Washington, he began to see that grim personal experience was merely an instance of disastrous regional history. And he began to wonder whether the personal and historical scars could have been avoided.

He arrived at a somewhat qualified affirmative. Ignorance, selfishness, greed — plain human cussedness — are the constants of history. Every recorded place has had its share of them, and all dismay over the failures of the past must be qualified by the admission that we are imperfect beings in an imperfect world. But the West, Stegner insists, has had more than its fair share of human cussedness. The question is, why? One factor, as we have observed, has been the enduring and enduringly inaccurate myth of the West as a never-never land of opportunity and riches. That myth provoked positive qualities such as independence and initiative; but it thrived on blindness to fact, stimulated avarice, and fostered "an unprecedented personal liberty, an atomic individualism, in a country that experience says can only be successfully tamed and lived in by a high degree of cooperation" (19). Moreover, the pioneer's virtues and vices were usually supplemented by what Stegner has described as "a kind of social cowardice."[2] The man who failed to prosper elsewhere went West. He was going somewhere, but he was also running from frustration and personal failure. And running became a regional habit, almost a tradition. The result is a history of ghost towns, abandoned mines, forgotten homesteads. Too often the combination of myth, aridity, individualism, and social cowardice has issued in a nightmare of dust.

A true Westerner, Stegner finds ample room for hope. Though the scars are deep, developments in recent years have altered past patterns and promise to avert serious wounds in the future. Hundreds of millions of Western acres are federally owned and operated, at least temporarily insulated against private exploitation. The spirit of conservation — which Stegner has done a great deal to encourage — has become more widespread since the end of World War II, and its impact has been salutary. Even in a state so overpopulated and industrialized as California there is some hope — provided, of course, that foresight is brought to the resolution of public and private differences. That distinctive cultural and social traditions have failed to flourish is regrettable. But that such patterns of regional stability may yet emerge is challenging and exciting. The past notwithstanding, Stegner believes that the West still "has a chance to create a society to match its scenery" (38).

Scenery is the substance of the personal memories in *The Sound of Mountain Water*. As an "Overture" to the essays, Stegner recalls his first visit to the Yellowstone country in 1920. He remembers himself as a boy just in off the prairie, for whom "it was pure delight to be where the land lifted in peaks and plunged in canyons." At the center of that memory is the Yellowstone River itself:

By such a river it is impossible to believe that one will ever be tired or old. Every sense applauds it. Taste it, feel its chill on the teeth: it is purity absolute. Watch its racing current, its steady renewal of force: it is transient and eternal. And listen again to its sounds: get far enough away so that the noise of falling tons of water does not stun the ears, and hear how much is going on underneath — a whole symphony of smaller sounds, hiss and splash and gurgle, the small talk of side channels, the whisper of blown and scattered spray gathering itself and beginning to flow again, secret and irresistible, among the wet rocks. (42–43)

That first, almost audible, marvelously rendered experience of mountain water takes us to the heart of what Stegner values in the West. The place itself — how it looks and smells and sounds and feels. That is the heart of it. Little wonder that he, like Wordsworth on Westminster Bridge more than a century before, should have found himself a little out of love with people when the reverie had passed.

Try to imagine London without people. For that matter, imagine most countryside without people. The mind remains blank. Most countryside and London require people; in some sense they *are* people. Now try to imagine the Grand Canyon full of people. Equally blank. Like much Western scenery, the Grand Canyon is best seen, and only imaginable, without people. Western scenery is awesome, remote, inaccessible; its spaces obscure humans; it has the look of eternity about it. Introduce people and you forfeit the real thrill. On the other hand, admit, as all good democrats must, that people have a right to be there; indeed, admit that they should be there, for it is an inspiring sight. Such is the painful dilemma of Wallace Stegner, a democrat who loves Western scenery.

The personal memories in *The Sound of Mountain Water* represent Stegner's more or less successful attempt to reconcile himself to Western people *in* Western landscapes. Basic ambivalences generate a mixture of tones. At times he celebrates what is eloquent and familiar and apparently permanent in nature. At other moments he is less positive. He admits that Lake Powell is a splendid recreational facility, that the shoreline is lovely and the water-skiers tolerable, but he cannot forget that the surface of the lake rests several hundred feet above the floor of Glen Canyon, once an exquisite stretch of the Colorado River, now impounded by the Glen Canyon Dam. A packhorse trip into Havasu Canyon inspires comparisons with Shangri-la and Xanadu, but the knowledge that increased tourism threatens the stability of the canyon's Indian culture is cause for genuine concern. It is to Stegner's credit that he confronts the wilderness paradox as squarely and articulately as he does. On the one hand, there are the claims of an expanding urban society anxious to get away from it all. Lake Powell and Havasu Canyon serve public interests; indeed, they create public health. On the other hand, there is a wilderness whose value is directly proportional to the relative absence of people. In Glen Canyon, possibly even in Havasu Canyon, the human touch need not be fatal. Nonetheless, when people appear in large numbers, something is lost. Inevitably, the rational democrat compromises with the romantic solitary, but not without regret. As Stegner puts it, "in gaining the lovely and the usable, we have given up the incomparable" (128).

Lake Powell may be acceptable, but other varieties of exploitation are not. The shores of Lake Tahoe, cluttered with tasteless cottages and casinos, epitomize for Stegner the human violation of nature's vulnerable serenity. Perhaps we have grown accustomed to Tahoe, or perhaps we avoid it — even the thought of it. But what of the desecration of less familiar landscapes? Can we get accustomed to, or forget, the billboards and junk shops that proliferate even in remote regions of the West? Stegner cannot. Billboards and junk shops make him angry. Anger, imperfectly submerged in broad, relentless irony, is the principal source of energy in "The Land of Enchantment," his sharpest assault on the human abuse of nature. The Land of Enchantment is — or used to be — New Mexico. "Everything is as it was, except that the enchantment has been improved and modernized" (137). What was desert has become gas stations and motels and roadside zoos with Gila monsters, rattlesnakes, mangy coyotes, and boa constrictors! The eye falls on the black silhouette of a jackrabbit. A mile or so down the highway there is another, this time bigger. Pretty soon there are enormous wooden jackrabbits everywhere. What does it mean? Why, that we are approaching "the Jack Rabbit Trading Post, of course" (140). Signs mean business. Business means people — lots of people. And it is difficult to fault Stegner's angry insistence that lots of people have no business putting up signs all over the wilderness.

In spite of it all, Stegner remains hopeful. Much of the most beautiful wilderness has been irreparably damaged, but cooperation and common sense can save what remains. Perhaps that kind of hope is no more than wishful thinking. Perhaps the wooden jackrabbits and plastic palaces will prevail. But, Stegner insists, man is very much the product of place, and the West is an optimistic place. "It has a shine on it; despite its mistakes, it isn't tired" (37). He is confident that time and experience will cause Westerners to recognize that the wilderness is an essential part of their heritage. If that happens, there will be plenty of room for hope, for then they will resent the artificial jackrabbits and plastic palaces as much as Stegner does.

Historical and personal memories finally prompt Stegner to

reflect on the ways of remembering. In three crucial essays — "Born a Square," "History, Myth, and the Western Writer," and "On the Writing of History" — he considers the personal and cultural conditions which confront Western writers. In the first two essays, he confines himself to Western novelists who, whether they like it or not, are born in a box with traps at both ends: the "box is booby-trapped at one end by an inadequate artistic and intellectual tradition, and at the other end by the coercive dominance of attitudes, beliefs, and intellectual fads and manners destructive of his own" (170). On one side, the Western novelist is handicapped by the fact that his region does not provide him with clear patterns and precedents. Unlike the East and the South, the West has not yet discovered what is usable in its past. On the other side, he finds himself an unfashionable provincial; an innocent, an advocate of the American Dream, he is not "at home in a literary generation that appears to specialize in despair, hostility, hypersexuality, and disgust" (171). To escape from the box, advises Stegner, the Western novelist must discover and articulate the connections between past and present. Otherwise he will fall prey either to the Scylla of nostalgia for a mythical, heroic past or to the Charybdis of rejecting the past for a cynical, desperate present. What we need is a Western William Faulkner, a writer who can avoid nostalgia and cynicism by exploring regional continuities; and, Stegner concludes, "I might even try myself" (200).

In "On the Writing of History," Stegner admits that he has already tried. In making the effort he has learned that a middle course between history and fiction, Clio and Calliope, has been the best protection against Scylla and Charybdis. Like prose fiction, history deals with persons, places, and events; some of the best of it takes vivid narrative form; it is not a science, but a branch of literature. Like history, novels reflect society and "may have an almost-historical value as record" (205). With Bernard DeVoto as his model, and with some of his own books as examples, Stegner defends what he calls "the middle ground" between Clio and Calliope. He doubts that any of his attempts to fuse fiction and history — *The Preacher and the Slave, Beyond the Hundredth Meridian, The Gathering of Zion,* and *Wolf Willow* — has been totally successful, but he is confident that the Faulkner of the West will have to create a similar, if more successful, fusion. Cold Western facts are not enough. Western fictions are too often misleading fabrications. But the imaginative rendering of Western persons, places, and events — "the middle ground"— should help to unveil those continuities between past and present which have remained obscure. We will chart and evaluate Stegner's course toward "the middle ground" in most of the discussion that follows.[3]

II *Mormons*

It may be that the best history is written by men who control a manageable maximum of information, and who bring enthusiasm, but not strong prepossessions, to bear on that information. They are in a good position to write interesting, objectively and imaginatively accurate history. If this is the case, then Wallace Stegner's situation as historian has been less than ideal. His facts have been plentiful and manageable enough, but they have been drawn from, or directly related to, Stegner's personal experience; and it is difficult, not to say impossible, to recount what is personal without strong prepossessions.

Stegner's historical topic is the West. More specifically, his topic is that region he knows best, the Rocky Mountain West. At the center of Western history is the land problem, and, as we have noted, the crux of the land problem has been water. For the most part Westerners have abused the land, principally through their misuse of radically limited water resources. According to Stegner, the typical Westerner, through either ignorance, greed, or both, has taken a get-rich-quick attitude to the environment. He has mined, grazed, logged, and planted with an eye to rapid personal profit, but in blindness to the fact that almost all of these activities are destructive in arid country unless they are carefully regulated. This typical, ruggedly individualistic Westerner, has been looking for the Big Rock Candy Mountain. In most cases, he has failed to find it. But the price of his failure has been widespread human suffering, exploitation and desecration of the land, and a pernicious romanticization of the rugged individualist. This typical Westerner is Bo Mason, the fictionalized George Stegner. He is also a Gentile in the land of the Saints.

Exceptions to the destructive pattern of Western history have been all too rare. There is the feminine alternative of permanence and cooperation, personified in Elsa Mason. But so far men have dominated the region beyond the hundredth meridian; women's voices have been lost in the clamor. A more important exception is the history of the Mormons. Like the typical Westerner, the Mormon was a personal experience for Stegner long before he was a historical type. But, by the time he left Salt Lake, Stegner must have recognized the Mormon community as a positive social and historical antidote to what afflicted East End. In later years, he would adopt Salt Lake as his home, and he would point to the Mormons as a potent exception to rugged individualism and its place in the general development of the West. This process of fusing personal experience with historical fact — under the pressure of strong prepossessions — took its first important nonfictional expression in *Mormon Country,* published in 1942.

Mormon Country opens with a dramatization, from the point of view of a rural teenage girl, of a "Mutual." The "Mutual," a weekly event in most Mormon Wards, is a gathering of local believers for expressions of faith, instruction in right living, and some good clean fun. Stegner's brief fiction is designed to catch the essence of Mormonism in a glance. The scene is set in mountain country: Mormons are basically a rural people. Among other things, the "Mutual" honors Heber Christianson, who is leaving on a mission to South America: Mormonism is an international movement. There is praying at the meeting, along with admonitions to avoid the devil drink and the wicked weed: the Mormons are a pious and virtuous people. But there is also plenty of laughing, singing, and dancing: the Mormons are a robust, fun-loving people. If we come away impressed with Mormon solidarity and cohesiveness, we have grasped most of the point. It remains to reflect that such social unity is not typically American, and we have it all. "It is participation," says Stegner, "shrewdly calculated and carefully nurtured, that maintains the group spirit and the Mormon belief in the small towns of Zion long after one would have expected the American system to dilute and destroy it."[4]

Part I — about the first two-thirds — of *Mormon Country* is a sequence of short chapters devoted to making concrete and specific those elements in Mormon history and culture which have combined to create the solidarity of the "Mutual." There is the land itself, remote, apparently barren; but as Brigham Young saw, it was also a sanctuary hundreds of miles from the persecuting Gentiles. Common purpose led to the discovery that irrigation and hard work could make the wasteland productive. Almost from the moment the Mormons arrived in 1847, they knew what the typical Westerner has learned the hard way — that cooperative use of limited water is the key to agricultural success in arid country. The Mormon town, modeled on the Heavenly City, is laid out in ten-acre blocks; each block has twenty half-acre lots; each lot contains one house set exactly twenty-five feet from the street; and the streets are a uniform eight rods wide. In the villages of Zion, orderly and spacious, we do not find the "derailed dining cars and false-fronted stores and rubbish-strewn vacant lots and desolate, treeless, grassless yards" of towns like East End: "The Gentiles often built that kind of town, in the Mormon Country and elsewhere; the Mormons practically never did" (28).

The Mormon town plan is an instance of the subordination of individual to group interests that Stegner sees as the key to the Mormons' solidarity and to their successful experiment on the arid frontier. Collective behavior of this kind is the result of widespread submission to central authority. Incessant persecution forced consolidation and generated a firm group identity. Strong leadership —·from Joseph Smith until 1844, and from Brigham Young until 1877 — fostered a still vital tradition of obedience. Politically a theocracy, the early Mormon empire, stretching far and wide in the intermountain region, was a totally authoritarian system with Brigham Young, prophet and dictator, at the center. Dissent was a perilous business. Brigham's private army, the Nauvoo Legion, and a ruthlessly effective secret police, made sure of that. The organization of smaller segments of the society — towns, religious units, families — mirrored the ironclad authoritarianism of the state as a whole. From top to bottom, there was nothing democratic about it.

Although the Mormons were internally a seamless robe, not even a remote desert could insulate them against incursions from the outside. It is in tones of regret that Stegner chronicles the dilution of the Mormon ethos. At almost every stage the gradual but unrelenting process involved the encroachment of the Gentile and of his god, Mammon. 1848 brought the Treaty of Guadalupe Hidalgo, which put Zion on the map of the United States. At almost the same time the discovery of gold in California brought hordes of Gentiles through the desert. Brigham Young wanted statehood and the measure of independence that came with it; instead, in 1850, the region was designated the Territory of Utah. Federal officials arrived. Hostilities followed: the Mountain Meadows Massacre of

Gentiles in 1857; the so-called Mormon War in the same year. In both incidents the Saints prevailed, but in both their entanglement with the outsider became more of a reality. Federal politics and Eastern dollars assured that the entanglement would grow tighter and deeper. Statehood came in 1896, but it came only with the outlawing of plural marriage. Almost fifty years later, as Stegner wrote the conclusion to the Mormon section of his book, the process of dilution seemed all but complete. "The Mormon Country is not yet Heaven on Earth, and it no longer really expects to be. It is every year more and more like any other state in the union" (235).

Part II, "The Might of the Gentile," looks at the invader. Stegner concedes that only *most* of the Gentiles have been bad for Mormondom. Jedediah Smith had a vision, and a short but honorable life. John Wesley Powell understood the land and almost succeeded in saving it. Earl Douglass, the paleontologist, "was as enthusiastic a pioneer and as dedicated a spirit as any Saint in the sandrock country" (305). And, he admits, there have been some bad Mormons. Butch Cassidy was the son of a pious Mormon, and several members of the Wild Bunch were broken branches of Zion. But the general picture is pretty clear and straightforward. The Mountainmen came to decimate the beaver and bison, to guzzle liquor, to chase squaws. The miners came to gut the land. The railroaders came in 1869 to exploit the market; they opened the West and thereby sealed the Mormons' fate. Finally, the cattlemen came to raise beef for Eastern markets and to lure young Mormon lads from the fold. Each wave of Gentiles came for something, got it, and departed. Behind them they left a Mormon culture that was slowly but ineluctably altered by each new assault.

Stegner's portrait of the invader could hardly be more negative. Rafael Lopez, a miner and a murderer, is "the apotheosis of the spirit of the mining camps, an animal with only a varnish of domestication over him." The Mormon, on the other hand, "is above all else a domesticated animal" (279–80). Bingham, a mining town that has managed to survive, has done so only because its inhabitants, when sober, decided that cooperation would make them richer than would quarreling. Thanks in no small part to the arrival of large numbers of Saints, the town of Bingham had achieved a semblance of order by 1942. But the force for change was money. That is why the Gentiles came; that is why they stayed. Mammon wins out in Zion.

We can call *Mormon Country* history only if we define that term quite liberally. Fictional dramatization is not usually found in history books, but Stegner employs it frequently and with good results. Most history proceeds in something like chronological fashion and attempts to be comprehensive, if not exhaustive. This book is thematic in its organization and carefully selective in its content. But to remark that *Mormon Country* is not like most history is merely to point out that it is something else: it is probably best described as somewhat informal, comparative social history. Most of the critics who reviewed the book thirty years ago praised its sympathetic and apparently accurate portrait of Mormon life. We are inclined to agree. Especially in his descriptions of rural Mormondom, Stegner captures the simplicity, the determination, the quiet communion, and the essential serenity that can grow among humble men of common purpose. The scene is drawn with loving care, and it strikes us as true to life.

Having said that much, it remains to point out that Stegner's polarization of Mormon and Gentile is on the simplistic side and tends to distort our impression of both groups. At times the contrast becomes a case of good guys versus bad guys. True, there are decent Gentiles, but almost to a man their goodness is a function of their resemblance to Mormons. Again true, there are bad Mormons, but very few of them. We are impressed with benevolent Mormon entrepreneurs like Jesse Knight who was not above amassing fortunes in the mines but who turned his money "to social rather than personal uses" (204). But the picture would be more plausible if something were said of less neighborly Mormon capitalists and of the role of tightfisted Saints in the dilution of Brigham Young's dream. There is some discussion of polygamy, but Stegner's tendency is to dismiss it as a calculated reponse to the population shortage. Surely there was more than Empire in Brigham's eye! We hear nothing of the Saint's racism, and too little of the lusterless drudgery that was the portion of most Mormon women. It may be that Stegner's version of Mormon despotism is a trifle on the benevolent side, and that such despotism has more to do with what many visitors have found humorless in Zion than he is prepared to acknowledge. From this angle the assertion that "the deliberate, organized, regimented exploitation of the family spirit seems to me possible only in Mormondom" (175) may be mistaking oppression for a good thing. At the least, the point of view is extreme.

Lest our criticism seem equally extreme, let it be said that Stegner's errors are not factual but interpretive. In general, he expands upon what is attractive in Mormons, but he ignores or makes light of what is less agreeable. Just the opposite is the case in his treatment of the Gentiles. But that, after all, is not a very startling lapse in a young writer who has rejected the East End of his past and adopted the Salt Lake. We will do well to remember that *The Big Rock Candy Mountain* and *Mormon Country* were published in consecutive years. In both books Stegner weighs competing social and cultural alternatives, and in both books the scale falls heavily on the side of the Saints. But what is admissible as point of view in fiction turns up as bias in social history. Strong personal prepossessions are an asset in the novel but a weakness in ostensibly objective nonfiction.

The Gathering of Zion, published in 1964, attests to Stegner's continuing interest in the Saints. It also marks the achievement of something approaching impartiality in his attitude to the chosen people. In a preface to the bibliography, he anticipates charges of bias and defends himself against them by outlining the sentiments and assumptions that form his point of departure. He writes "as a non-Mormon but not a Mormon-hater." He is not a believer, but he does not quarrel with those who are. He avoids theological subtleties except when they are essential to accurate descriptions of people and their behavior. For the organization of the Mormon Church, he has respect; of its hierarchy, he is suspicious. He acknowledges "warm admiration" for "the everyday virtues of the Mormons," claims hundreds of them as good friends, and admits that Salt Lake City is close to his heart. To Stegner, too much Mormon history is partisan propaganda and outright distortion written by insiders; he describes himself as "an outsider" with no ambition "to whitewash the Mormon tribal crimes, which were as grievous as their wrongs."[5] In short, he has attempted to be as fair as possible.

Most readers will feel that Stegner has succeeded. In part, his success results from a clear definition of subject. Subtitled *The Story of the Mormon Trail,* the book chronicles the overland migration of pioneer Saints. The space: fourteen hundred miles of rugged terrain between the Mississippi and the Great Salt Lake Valley. The time: the twenty-two years between the expulsion of the Mormons from Nauvoo in 1846 and the completion of the transcontinental railroad in 1869. About fifty thousand souls felt compelled to make the perilous journey. Indians were not much of a problem; but the elements, inadequate supplies, and Gentiles were. For many, the trip began in Liverpool, where thousands of English and northern European converts, most of them poor, responded to the pull of new hope in a new world. The vast majority got through, though they were gaunt and parched and weak-kneed when they reached Zion. They succeeded, according to Stegner, because they were "the most systematic, organized, disciplined . . . pioneers in our history" (6).

When absolutely necessary, Stegner leaves the trail. Without some discussion of Joseph Smith's terrible fate, the construction of the Temple at Nauvoo, or the Mormon War, the story would be less than complete. But for the most part, he confines himself to the trail and to the people who crossed it. During the winter of 1846, fugitive Saints were scattered across the mid-West between Illinois and Missouri. The following spring, with Brigham Young in firm command, a small party made its way across the plains to the eastern slope of the Rockies. On July 22, 1848, through a notch in the mountains, the travelers had their first glimpse of the Great Salt Lake. Two days later their leader arrived. "This is the right place," he said, and they took him at his word. Like many in the party, Brigham was down with a fever that caught them during the final weeks of the journey. Still, theirs was a comparatively effortless prairie crossing. Later parties would travel without the benefit of Brigham's genius for organization and discipline. They would quarrel, some would give up, others would suffer, hundreds would die. Bad planning and worse weather took the lives of more than two hundred Saints who set out across the plains pushing handcarts toward Zion in 1856. During that year particularly, rescue was "a major theme" (97).

The strengths of *The Gathering of Zion* are manifold. Stegner's characteristic talent for evoking landscape is everywhere in evidence; our experience of the trail is vivid and concrete. He tells his story very well, and this story would be good even if told badly. His portraits of individual pioneers — Daniel W. Jones, a tough, honest, gun-slinging Saint, and Ursulia Hascall, so optimistic she would have come out in a hail storm "wondering if it wasn't a good time to make up a nice freezer of ice cream" (72), among many others — are indispensable masterpieces of compression and telling detail. Most crucial of all, what emerges as bias in *Mormon Country* has here become a cooler, more detached, finally more plausible assessment of the Latter-Day Saints. Their record is impressive. The facts indicate that success was the fruit of virtues peculiarly abundant among Mormon pioneers. But it is clearer in this book that fanaticism had its place beside cooperation on the road to Salt Lake: "Suffering, endurance, discipline, faith, brotherly and sisterly charity, the qualities so thoroughly celebrated by Mormon writers, were surely well distributed among them, but theirs also was a normal amount of human cussedness, vengefulness, masochism, backbiting, violence, ignorance, selfishness, and gullibility" (12-13). Humor begets acuity in the comparison of the pioneer Saints to "a herd of rather amiable musk oxen" (300); and humor, rather broadly defined as good-natured detachment, is the quality in *The Gathering of Zion* that makes it such a decided improvement upon *Mormon Country*. Informed, imaginative, dramatic to good effect, superbly written, Stegner's narrative moves away from personal bias; accordingly, it moves toward "the middle ground."

III *Gentiles*

Wallace Stegner's ambivalence, even hostility, to the Gentile record in the West admits some exceptions. Abraham Lincoln has his esteem, as does Mark Twain, his favorite American writer. *Beyond the Hundredth Meridian* (1954) is Stegner's tribute to another great Westerner, John Wesley Powell. The book is a biography, but only in the special sense that it chronicles not a personal life but a career. Stegner elects to present Powell as "the personification of an ideal of public service that seems peculiarly a product of the American experience."[6] This crucial decision was undoubtedly a wise one, for it allowed Stegner to treat Powell as an ideal type, as a model alternative to the dominant patterns of Western thought and experience. The personal is subordinated to the prophetic.

Beyond the Hundredth Meridian is the longest, the most scholarly, perhaps the best written, and certainly the most valuable of Stegner's contributions to historical nonfiction. It was many years — about six — in the works. We are inclined to agree with other critics who have been almost unanimous in their conviction that Stegner's time was well spent. Stegner "has added a basic book to the small shelf of books that give history basic knowledge of Western experience" (xxiii), says Bernard DeVoto in his introduction to the volume. Joseph Henry Jackson praised it as "the kind of synthesis that constitutes history in the finest and most valuable sense."[7] Few critics have disagreed with this view.

We should not be surprised that *Beyond the Hundredth Meridian* opens with a dichotomy. Just as surely as East End is the opposite of Salt Lake, the Honorable William Gilpin is the antitype to Powell. The first territorial governor of Colorado, experienced but utterly deceived, Gilpin was a tireless promoter of the myth that the West was a pastoral Canaan. The principal contents of what Stegner personifies as the Gilpin mind are perfectly simple and simply wrong. Because of abundant rainfall, ample artesian reserves, soil of unprecedented fertility, and a uniformly temperate climate, the West was an enormous garden: "Agriculture was effortless: no forests needed clearing, manual tillage was not required, even the use of the plow was not essential, so eager were seeds to germinate in this Paradise" (4). In the few places where the soil was inadequate, there the Gilpin mind found limitless stores of minerals and precious metals. Completion of the transcontinental railroad would convert pioneer hardship to high-speed luxury. The Gilpin mind envisioned hundreds of millions of Americans finding happiness and prosperity in the land of infinite promise. Such was the romantic myth of the American West in 1868: bizarre, potent, pernicious.

At the other extreme was the mind of John Wesley Powell, who "operated by common sense, had a faith in facts, and believed in system" (6). Powell was one of the first to recognize the full implications of the fact that aridity was the limiting characteristic of the West. From that fact, and from long, loving experience in that region, he drew important inferences: limited water meant limited settlement; aridity made irrigation essential to cultivation; cooperation among small farmers was the key to optimum water use; federal regulation of the public domain was the only sure protection against political and private exploitation of a vulnerable landscape. In sum, the Gilpin myth, with its optimistic overtones of Arcadian Manifest Destiny, bore with it the seeds of regional disaster. Against heavy odds, but with some success, Powell made it his life's work to avert such disaster.

He started out by getting an education. It passed for education in the West, at any rate; in the East it would have been called deprivation. Born in Mount Morris, New York, in 1834, the eldest son of an immigrant Methodist preacher, Powell had what Stegner calls a "homemade education" (8). Westward wandering was a part of it. At first it was family migration from Mount Morris to Jackson, Ohio; onward to a frontier farm in rural Wisconsin; finally to Bonus Prairie, Illinois. Later, during his teens, Powell took off on summer trips up and down the Mississippi River. It was instruction in rivers, farms, frontier towns. For the rest of it, education was the Bible, hard work, a few books, a timely mentor, inadequate colleges, optimism, democratic idealism. What emerged was a self-made naturalist with interests and some learning in several of the natural sciences. In April, 1861, after a brief term as secretary of the Illinois State Natural History Society, Powell volunteered as a private in the Union Army. He resigned in January, 1865, having gained the rank of major, but having lost his right arm in the bloody encounter at Shiloh. Two years and a couple of teaching jobs later found him the curator of the Illinois Natural History Society museum in Bloomington. From that august elevation he turned his eyes to the West.

With little money, with ill-sorted assistants, but with fierce determination, Powell devoted the next decade to exploration in the Plateau Province of the Rocky Mountains. A year or so of reconnaissance brought him to Green River, Wyoming, a junction of the Union Pacific Railroad. There, on May 24, 1869, with four boats and a handful of men, he pushed off on his most famous adventure, the navigation of the most treacherous stretches of the Green and Colorado Rivers. The sixty pages that Stegner expends on this incredible journey are some of the most exciting that are likely to be found in all American history. There is the perilous exhilaration of men in small boats riding mountainous waves through narrow canyons past boulders the size of a house. Disaster is a constant: boats are splintered; Powell clings one-handed to a canyon wall; three of the party withdraw at Separation Rapid to meet Shivwits braves and sudden death. After more than three months of wet rations, brutal alterations of heat and cold, exhausting work and too little sleep, two of the original four boats drifted out of the Grand Canyon to safety. It was an extraordinary accomplishment. Suddenly Powell was a public figure with legitimate claims on public support.

In 1870, Congress appropriated ten thousand dollars as support for additional exploration of the Colorado River. It was a small start, but that was all Powell needed. Years later his work would bear the ponderous title, United States Geographical Survey of the Rocky Mountain Region, J. W. Powell in Charge; but, for the moment, titles were unimportant. It was sufficient that there was an opportunity to get back to the field and a springboard to power in a government more than ever preoccupied with science.

Space does not permit anything like a full description of Powell's activities and offices during the culminating decades of his public life. The survey was a central interest, though as years passed he delegated increasing responsibility to assistants. More and more he spent his time in Washington, urging appropriations, befriending Congressmen, influencing policy, and writing the *Report on the Exploration of the Colorado River of the West and its Tributaries* (1875) and the *Report on the Geology of the Eastern Portion of the Uinta Mountains* (1876). Peaceful encounters with Indians and an awareness that their cultures were collapsing stimulated what was to be Powell's lifelong interest in ethnology. Scattered as all of these activities seem, they took rise from the man's compelling ambition "to prevent the spread of misconceptions about the West" (176).

In 1877, the Powell survey, along with the three other Western surveys — led by Ferdinand Hayden, Clarence King, and George Wheeler — fell under the scrutiny of a Congress bent on reform. Internal rivalries, combined with wasteful duplication, resulted in the proposal to unify the surveys under a single leader who would be responsible to the Secretary of the Interior. Powell was in favor of consolidation if the right leader — Clarence King — were chosen. Working skillfully behind the scenes, and with the powerful support of the National Academy of Sciences, Powell had his way: King took charge of the survey, and Powell contented himself with the Bureau of Ethnology.

Beyond mere bureaucracy, however, Powell was convinced that the laws regulating Western development were the offspring of the Gilpin mind. Premised on the myth of inexhaustible resources, geared to encourage individualism, the laws were productive of little save conflict, monopoly, exploitation, and waste. Powell responded with the *Report on the Lands of the Arid Region of the United States,* which he presented to Carl Schurz, the new Secretary of the Interior, in April, 1878. According to Stegner, the document was revolutionary, "a denial of almost every cherished fantasy and myth associated with the Westward migration and the

American dream of the Garden of the World" (212). Its point of departure was Western aridity. Its proposals — parceling of land by federal agencies, surveying based on water resources, cooperative irrigation farming, to name a few — represented a rational adjustment to limited water beyond the hundredth meridian. Schurz was sympathetic, but Congress went along with Gilpin. Powell's revolution would have to wait.

The final third of *Beyond the Hundredth Meridian* is the record of Powell's steady rise to power and influence and of his final defeat. In 1881, he replaced Clarence King at the head of the Geological Survey. The task — to survey and map the entire nation — was enormous. During the thirteen years before his retirement, Powell got as far with the job, and did it as well, as any man could have. More important, as head of this survey he was at once an aggressive advocate and an impressive symbol of government-supported science in areas where private initiative would jeopardize the public interest. His power reached its zenith in the years following 1886 when arctic winters and parching drought left portions of the arid region almost uninhabitable. Powell convinced Congress that an irrigation survey was essential and that, until it was completed, further settlement was an invitation to even worse disaster. For the future, he proposed to terminate agricultural expansion in the West except in areas where irrigation was feasible. By 1890, Powell's revolution seemed complete. Congress repealed existing land laws and closed the public domain. Further settlement would wait on the irrigation survey.

Powell's revolution was the product of science, reason, and common sense. That may help account for the fact that his revolution was also very brief. Western politics, Western venality, Western mythology, and the curious American attachment to the doctrine of laissez-faire were the chief antagonists. They merged in Big Bill Stewart, a senator from Nevada and a new incarnation of the Honorable William Gilpin. In House and Senate Appropriation Committee hearings during the summer of 1890, Stewart and his followers launched a brutal, sometimes baldly *ad hominem* attack. The survey was moving too slowly; Powell had overlooked enormous artesian resources; maps were unnecessary; Powell had misused funds; he was power hungry; he was not to be trusted; the whole affair smelled of government paternalism. Powell, resolute and dignified, insisted that "it would be almost a criminal act" to allow "hundreds of thousands of people to establish homes where they cannot maintain themselves" (333). Subsequent history has been bitter testimony to the accuracy of his position. But Congress in 1890 was either shortsighted, indifferent, or both. The public domain was reopened, and Powell's budget was slashed by over five hundred thousand dollars. It was "the beginning of the end of his public career" (337).

Powell resigned from the Geological Survey in 1894. Eight years later he died. The details of his decline are unimportant. What does matter is Powell's example. The ideals that informed his work — dedication to public service, scientific objectivity, conservation, government policy directed to public rather than private interests — were not unique in the Gilded Age, but they were rare and seldom found in combination. Generally speaking, his analysis of the problems in the arid region and the solutions he proposed were correct. Indeed, the years since his death have witnessed widespread adoption of Powell's ideas. Nonetheless, the triumph of reasonable land policy in the West was no more complete in 1953, when Stegner completed the biography, than it is today. Viewed in this light, *Beyond the Hundredth Meridian* shows no sign of losing its relevance. More than history, it is prophecy; it tells us what happened, what is happening, and what will continue to happen. It is greatly to Stegner's credit, but also, we have no doubt, to his dismay, that the message of this important biography is unlikely to become obsolete.

In the spring of 1953, not long after he completed his study of Powell, Stegner began work on what was to become *Wolf Willow*. The book began as a proposal to the Wenner-Gren Foundation for Anthropological Research. Stegner had it in mind to compare three small towns — East End, Saskatchewan, Greensboro, Vermont, and a third on a Danish island in the south Baltic — where population had been more or less homogeneous and politics firmly democratic over a long stretch of time. Grant in hand, he spent the summer in East End and Greensboro doing research. The following spring, he was in Denmark for about four months. For several good reasons, however, the comparative study of village democracy was never written. Early on Stegner discovered that he was neither political scientist nor sociologist enough to do the job to his own satisfaction. Furthermore, whatever political speculation he engaged in quickly became personal and historical reflection. Finally, he discovered that East End was the town he wanted to write about.

Part history, part fiction, part autobiography, *Wolf Willow* is a structurally complicated, somewhat untidy production that almost works. The book seems to have developed as a collection of imperfectly related parts. The problem was to knit the parts into a coherent sequence. It was not until 1962, after nine years of sporadic writing and organizing, that Stegner finally allowed his manuscript to go to press. Most readers will agree that the parts of *Wolf Willow* are more successful than the whole.

The book is divided into four sections. The first, second, and fourth sections amount to an informal, selective, roughly chronological history of East End. Woven through the historical narrative, providing color and human interest, are the substantial strands of autobiography already noted. Making no pretense to total objectivity, Stegner writes in the first person. He is an amiable, sympathetic, even nostalgic, but nonetheless sharply critical observer of what was once his home town. It is pleasantly surprising to find that East End has a history; as a child he had assumed it had none. What he describes, or, more properly, discovers, is a kind of capsular version of frontier experience on the plains. In the main, he admits, the story is pretty depressing. The myth of a Western Paradise, gullibility, social cowardice, individualism, violence, drought — East End grew up under familiar conditions. The pattern of development has been equally familiar: in general, Gilpin has triumphed over Powell.

When Lewis and Clark passed south of the site of modern East End in 1805, they found little to give them pause. A generation later Indians stayed long enough to engage in bloody tribal warfare and to slaughter countless buffalo. They were followed by the *métis,* half French, half Indian, who were well adapted to the conditions of the region, but no match for young, westward-growing Canada. Surveyors established the boundary along the 49th parallel in 1874. It was a "very open and penetrable fence."[8] Fugitive Indians and whiskey traders crossed the line to escape the harsh treatment called American justice. But traders and Indians found plenty to quarrel about, even in their sanctuary. Canada responded with the Mounted Police, who came to impose law and order, and to watch over the decline of the Indian culture.

The Mounties "had more authority and were generally more to be trusted and easier to get on with than the blue-coated American cavalry, and much more to be trusted than Montana sheriffs or marshals or posses" (98). Above all, they were effective — so effective, in fact, that by 1880 cattlemen felt safe enough to move their herds into the area. But the Mounties could not protect them from winters like the one in 1906–1907 which decimated the stock and drove most of the ranchers out. Homesteaders followed, settled around the new town of East End, and were little more successful than their predecessors. With George Stegner, many left; others stuck. Some of them, like Corky Jones and Bill Anderson, were still around when Wallace Stegner returned in 1953. He found a few old friends, some trees where there had been none, a few signs of local development. In the final tally, however, the town had failed. In all likelihood it will continue to be what it has always been, "marginal or submarginal in its community and cultural life" (306).

Stegner acknowledges that in *Wolf Willow* he "occasionally warped fact a little in order to reach for the fictional or poetic truth" that he ranks "a little above history" (307). In other words, by dramatizing Western persons and events he has attempted to reach "the middle ground." He comes closest to achieving it in the two stories that form the third section of the book. Founded upon verbal and written records of the disastrous winter of 1906–1907, Stegner's historically based fictions are designed to take the reader beyond fact to an almost concrete "feel" for catastrophe on the frozen, lonely plains. Facts alone would fail to catch the complex texture of cowboy life, the subtle mix and interplay of courage, callousness, self-reliance, prejudice, solitude, comradeship. We will come as close to seeing it as it actually was, says Stegner, if we look "through the eyes of some tenderfoot, perhaps someone fresh from the old country, a boy without the wonder rubbed off him and with something to prove about himself" (138).

This is not the place to summarize the plot of "Genesis," a tale in which a young Englishman learns "that what would pass for heroics in a softer world was only chores" (219) on a snowbound prairie. The second story, "Carrion Spring," exposes us to the stench of rotting cattle after the thaw in 1907. Surrounded by numberless carcasses, a frontier wife submits to her husband's courageous but foolhardy insistence that they try again to raise cattle in Saskatchewan. Individually, the stories rank with Stegner's best; they lend signal confirmation to his argument that fictional renderings of the past can sometimes bring us closer to the truth than historical fact. Viewed as a sequence, however, they display in an extreme form the structural discontinuity that characterizes *Wolf Willow* as a whole.

"Genesis," as Stegner promised, is narrated from the tenderfoot's point of view. It gets us about as close to the hardships of cowboy life as we are likely to come. But the point of view shifts abruptly when we turn to "Carrion Spring." An omniscient narrator takes over, discourses for a few pages on the trials of frontier weather, and then, almost as abruptly as he appeared, vanishes. The story that follows is told from a woman's point of view. These sudden shifts, which mar the unity of the sequence, probably result from the fact that Stegner constructed *Wolf Willow* out of parts written over a long period of time. Originally a story called "The Wolfer" was to follow "Genesis," but it was finally rejected on the reasonable grounds that its point of view was in jarring contrast to what preceded.[9] As an alternative Stegner introduced the omniscient narrator as a transitional voice between "Genesis" and "Carrion Spring." As we have already indicated, the transition is not a smooth one, and the problem remains.

Structural problems notwithstanding, the short stories are the most effective chapters in *Wolf Willow*. Their excellence is symptomatic. Like Stegner's best historical nonfiction, *Beyond the Hundredth Meridian,* these historical fictions arise rather naturally out of their author's past. The material is familiar; the region is familiar; the characters are familiar; they capture Stegner's imagination and usually his approval. At the same time, the region, materials, and characters are sufficiently remote in time and space to allow cool scrutiny. Distance generates objectivity in Stegner without impairing his powers of invention. The twenty years that separate *Mormon Country* from *The Gathering of Zion* were two decades that Stegner spent away from Salt Lake; and this span of years helps to account for the superiority of the second book. Time tempered strong personal prepossessions, but left mind and memory free to search for the truth of "the middle ground."

CHAPTER 3

Literary Criticism and Short Fiction

I *The Critical Framework*

WALLACE Stegner learned many valuable lessons from Bernard DeVoto. He acquired his friend's respect for the "hard stuff" that informs all good writing, historical or otherwise. And he acquired DeVoto's respect for the literary techniques which bring the "hard stuff" of writing to life: an appropriate narrative voice, landscape description and character sketch, irony, hyperbole, and suspense. But despite this craftsmanlike admiration for tools, Stegner, like DeVoto, inherited the Westerner's almost constitutional aversion to literary criticism and other species of "beautiful thinking." Like DeVoto, Frost, and Twain before him, Stegner reserves his admiration for the leader rather than counterpuncher, the doer rather than talker, the worker — in Robert Frost's words — who can swing what he knows.

Accordingly, the canon of Stegner's literary criticism is short and unified, casual in its presentation, and almost self-consciously "professional" in its point of view. Throughout a forty-year career of unremitting productivity, Stegner has published only one extended piece of literary criticism, *The Writer in America.* This slim volume consists of seven short "3.2 literary essays," designed to provide a Japanese-speaking audience with a brief but comprehensive introduction to the mysteries of American fiction. Quite literally "small beer!" The rest of Stegner's critical canon stretches to about forty happily heterogeneous articles. Again, they are brief, pragmatic in approach, and deliberately directed to the nonscholarly world. Each of these articles is designed to achieve a single, concrete objective. Many intend to pass technical "tips" or professional chitchat on to fellow readers of *The Writer, College English,* and *Author and Journalist.* Others attempt to indoctrinate an audience of educated laymen by providing *Harper's,* the *Atlantic,* and the *Saturday Review* with surveys of contemporary fiction. As all the articles fulfill a specific function, they all avoid that posture of intellectual superiority which a native son of *The Literary Fallacy* was bound to eschew.

Not surprisingly, the major features of Stegner's critical stance are traditional, conservative, and commonsensical in their origins. They make their first appearance among Stegner's early, exploratory articles and continue, expanded but essentially unmodified, to form the substance of his later work. According to Stegner, as we have already observed, the creative process is no more and no less than the imposition of form upon personal experience. The fledgling writer begins with the people, places, and events of his own childhood, much as Stegner himself started out with the rich imagery and sensuous rhythms of East End germinating in his memory. But this is only the jumping-off place, the first step; next, the writer must discipline himself to the "dog work" of creation. He must sift the significant images from the insignificant, devise a meaningful action for his characters, imbue them with life, and then — by imposing a beginning, middle, and an end upon their activities — condemn them to what Hemingway called death.[1] In short, the writer must transform the chaos of memory into the orderliness of art and do so without offending his reader's sense of what is true to life.

This straightforward credo is alive throughout the entire range of Stegner's critical writing. In "The Making of Fiction," published by *The Rocky Mountain Review* in the fall of 1941, he argues that the transcription of reality presumed to be characteristic of fiction is more properly a "remaking": "We organize a story or a novelette or a novel not as it happened but as our imagination tells us it ought to happen. . . . The whole job of a writer of fiction is to make real dialogue into fictional dialogue, real characters into fictional characters, real places into fictional places."[2] Similarly, in "Teaching the Short Story," published by the University of California in the fall of 1965, Stegner begins by asserting that literary communication can be as intimate and personal as a connubial chat; but the bulk of his essay is nonetheless devoted to a discussion of formal considerations. As Stegner puts it, "the problem is form without loss of truth."[3] Remembered experience is meaningless without the mediation of the artist's impulse toward order.

The critic who values memory as much as Wallace Stegner is also likely to value the regional in American literature; for until the very recent past, the American experience was a regional experience.

The artist who thought deeply about the events of his own child-hood was sure to see himself as a New Englander, Southerner, Mid-westerner, or Westerner. This supposition is borne out in *The Writer in America;* here Wallace Stegner finds literary models in Mark Twain, Willa Cather, William Faulkner, and Robert Frost. If he fails sufficiently to appreciate the local genius of Nathaniel Hawthorne, Herman Melville, and Henry James, it is partly be-cause nineteenth-century New England can never seem like just another region to a boy from East End. As an American realist in the moral tradition of William Dean Howells, Stegner is unsympa-thetic to the heavy symbolism and metaphysical preoccupations characteristic of the New England mind. He makes great claims for regional literature, perhaps too great. For him it possesses a special piquancy virtually denied to works of a more international flavor. In Robert Frost's "Stopping by Woods on a Snowy Evening," for example, Stegner finds "The Americanisms are almost like a play-ful disguise meant to be penetrated, so that ... the two great literary effects of recognition and surprise can both be had — the recognition of the universal human spirit penetrating the initial dis-guise of the local manner."[4] Maybe so. In any case, less than a decade later, Stegner in effect admonishes the literary world to look sharp to its seasoning, for he finds regionalism fast disappearing from the American consciousness. In "West Coast: Region with a View," he wonders whether Washington, Oregon, and California share an "identifiable culture" and is forced to conclude that they do not.[5] By 1959, the West Coast is simply America, only more so.

But regionalism is not the only corollary to Stegner's espousal of the "personal heresy." If literature finds its wellspring in personal experience, then people, things, and places will surely assume a spe-cial importance denied to intangibles such as religion and ideology. "Ideas," says Stegner in *The Writer in America,* "are not the best *subject matter* for fiction. They do not dramatize well. They are rather a by-product, something the reader himself is led to formu-late after watching the story unfold.... They ought to haunt a piece of fiction as a ghost flits past an attic window after dark."[6] A sensible stance for a realist, but one difficult to maintain, given the grim social and economic inequities of modern life. Any writer who attempts to "remake" the experience of Depression America will surely find himself adopting a political viewpoint, if only by default. As the popular saying goes, "if you're not part of the solution, you're part of the problem." For Wallace Stegner, the "ghosts" haunting the house of fiction will occasionally assume a disturbing corporality.

A moralist as well as realist, Stegner has equally strong views about the thematic concerns appropriate to art, especially if that art aspires to greatness. For Stegner, great literature must inspire tolerance if not affection for the "damned human race," and inculcate resolute acceptance of this world and its problems. In "Is the Novel Done for?" he agrees that God is dead and the world in chaos but argues that this neither justifies self-pity nor abrogates individual responsibility. "If Newton, Darwin, Marx, and Freud constitute a grammar of living, our actual daily lives are the usage."[7] And in our daily lives we do assume free will, we do accept absolute ethical standards, and we do take responsibility for our actions. In short, men achieve affirmation not in ignorance of the pain of experience, but in spite of it.

Given this much, it is no surprise to find Joseph Conrad in Stegner's hierarchy of literary giants. Neither a regionalist nor a realist, Conrad is nevertheless a masterful explorer of the mysteries of human conduct — which Stegner defines as "the relation between an individual and a set of values." In "Variations on a Theme by Conrad," Stegner scrutinizes the "country-rector" code of values that informs the character, Lord Jim. He is perfectly prepared to acknowledge the inadequacies of Jim's code; especially within the context of a decadent maritime morality, it is a code that often appears "silly, romantic, and Boy Scout-ish" to the reader. But Stegner insists upon the significance of the code as a measuring rod for conduct. "It is capable of making everything else in Jim's life unimportant by comparison with his self-respect, and it can extort from him extremes of abnegation and sacrifice that may be silly and romantic but are also admirable."[8] Similarly, in "Robert Frost: 'A Lover's Quarrel with the World,'" it is the poet's "steady acceptance of consequences" that excites Stegner's admiration and respect. "Of course this is a dark poet," he concedes of Frost; "any poet worth his salt is dark. But what one hears almost everywhere else in our literature, the accent of self-pity, one never hears in him."[9]

In his dedication to *The Year of Decision: 1846,* Bernard DeVoto celebrated "the basic courage and honor in the face of adversity which we call gallantry."[10] Gallantry: that is as good a word as any to sum up Stegner's thematic requirements for fiction. And yet it is the kind of word that puts Stegner right where it placed DeVoto — in the double corner. Stegner's Western posture makes him congenitally uncomfortable with a notion like "artist" — "In its capital A form . . . the hallmark of that peculiarly repulsive sin of arrogance by which some practitioners of the arts retaliate for public neglect or compensate for personal inadequacy."[11] And yet the Western legacy of optimism and idealism makes Stegner an unabashed believer in the very "high seriousness" he is reluctant publicly to espouse. Like the rough-and-ready Forty-niner whose respect for gentility was inverse to his desire to practice it, Stegner maintains an outlander's faith in the educative, ennobling function of literature. How to resolve this conflict? Wallace Stegner chose the same compromise that Bernard DeVoto chose before him. DeVoto wrote under a half-dozen aliases. The pseudonym John August graced the serial entertainments he produced for fun and profit; his own name he reserved strictly for the "real stuff." Stegner does not use two names, but he does pursue a variety of literary objectives. Working as a journalist, he has produced hundreds of popular magazine articles — timely, informative, but intentionally ephemeral in their effect. In his role as a novelist, however, he has aspired to and often achieved the timelessness and universality characteristic of great art. The subject of the remainder of this chapter — Stegner's short fiction — is a case in point. Some of his tales were clearly designed as commercial entertainment; as such, they more than succeed, though they lie outside the province of this book. As we shall see, however, the majority of Stegner's short stories anticipate and compare well with the very best of his longer works.

II   *The Short Fiction: Two Personae, One Theme*

In the past four decades, Wallace Stegner has produced nearly fifty short stories. They have appeared in an impressive assortment of popular and scholarly publications. We find ten in *Harper's,* six in *Mademoiselle,* five in the *Atlantic Monthly,* and two or three each in *Collier's, Cosmopolitan, Esquire, Redbook,* the *Intermountain,* and *Virginia Quarterly Reviews.* Happily for the Stegner reader, over half of these tales — in general, the better half — have been republished in more permanent form. The first collection, *The Women on the Wall,* gathers together the best Stegner stories published from 1938 to 1946; the second, *The City of the Living,* includes those which appeared between 1947 and 1956.[12] Taken together, these two slim volumes constitute a microcosm of Stegner's development as an artist.

In the first place, both collections include a series of what we may call literary exercises — exploratory short stories, the best of which form the foundation for three of Stegner's major novels. "Two Rivers" and "The Colt," for example, describe critical incidents in the youth of Bruce Mason, chief protagonist of *The Big Rock Candy Mountain;* "Field Guide to the Western Birds" introduces Joe Allston, the cantankerous philosopher-hero of *All the Little Live Things.* But our microcosm metaphor also applies to these two collections on a second, more sophisticated level. The collected tales span the years 1938 through 1956 — years which brought their creator from youth to middle age. During this critical period, we can observe Wallace Stegner's characteristic point of view changing from that of a young boy and then young man like Bruce Mason to that of a middle-aged and finally elderly man like Joe Allston. Simultaneously, we find our author's preferred mode of narration moving from the third to the first person. Despite this gradual change in perspective, however, the major themes of Stegner's short fiction remain relatively the same: initiation, maturity, identity, in short, growing up — reconciliation or resignation, as the case may be. Perhaps these are simply the themes of all literature. After all, men are born to live, grow old, and die. But if they are themes that admit of infinite variation, they also lend a comforting continuity to the canon of Stegner's short fiction.

III *Brucie*

"The Chink" — written and published in 1940 — is one of the few tales of Stegner's Saskatchewan boyhood omitted from *The Big Rock Candy Mountain.* Like most of Stegner's fiction, it finds its source in personal experience; the germ of the story reappears as autobiographical fact in *Wolf Willow* almost twenty-five years after its first publication in fictionalized form. Let us return for a moment to East End, the very zenith of Stegner country. We will remember young Wallace in his small boy's paradise; Mah Jim and Mah Li, the two pig-tailed Chinese who glittered like jewels in that drab setting; and East End's harsh code which classified foreigners with other weaklings and which victimized both without mercy. Wallace Stegner remembered these things too, and all find their way into "The Chink."

The narrator of "The Chink" is given no forename, but he is clearly the youthful Wallace Stegner — a boy from Saskatchewan grown up enough to contemplate the meaning of his own experience. Bruce recreates for us his abortive childhood friendship with Mah Li, the younger and the gentler of East End's two-man Chinese community. Mah Jim ran the inevitable Chinese restaurant and impressed himself upon a childish imagination as the eagle-eyed proprietor of the candy counter. But Mah Li, when he was not doing the town laundry, grew vegetables and caught fish. A frontier boy like Brucie could hardly fail to admire his quiet control over nature. Bumblebees blundered into Mah Li's brow; butterflies rested comfortably on his shoulders. And, best of all, he tamed Brucie's injured magpie and taught it to mimic the boy's pidgin-English nickname — the family laundry mark, "0-5! 0-5!"

Despite these impressive skills, Mah Li remained an outsider to life in East End, even for a runt like Brucie who was not quite an insider himself. "Sometimes I catch myself remembering him in the same way I remember the black colt my father gave me when I was nine," Bruce recalls with shame in the opening paragraph of "The Chink." "I loved Mah Li as I loved the colt, but neither was part of the life that seemed meaningful at the time."[13] With his black queue, slanted eyes, and cream-colored complexion, Mah Li certainly looked like something more or less than human. Brucie knew that the two Chinese brothers were fair game for the cruel side of the local code of action. He had tweaked enough pigtails and snitched enough candy bars to be sure of that. But how was he to know they deserved to benefit from Whitemud's few positive values — friendship, courage, loyalty to one's mates? How indeed, except through sad experience.

Experience arrived with a vengeance one Halloween eve in October, 1918. In a town like East End, Halloween is a small boy's saturnalia. For one night of freedom, all rules are suspended, all roles reversed, and all adults — weak or strong — made the victims of pranks. Brucie and his cohorts decide to begin their mischief with a raid on Mah Jim's candy bars. But they are foiled in the attempt and retaliate with an even more elaborate assault. A well-disciplined boyish army, they stage a surprise attack on the brothers' privy, push it over, and are startled by a yelp from within. Mah Jim caught inside? As if to clinch the revenge, the biggest and boldest of the boys nails the privy door shut while his confused comrades stand by. Brucie begins to protest but loses his nerve and falls silent. As a marginal member of this army, an outsider not yet securely inside, he fears that protest will appear treason.

At this point, Nemesis intervenes in the form of the 1918 flu epidemic, the plague that ravaged East End along with much of the rest of North America. Its arrival puts a dramatic damper on the Halloween festivities; it also provides Brucie with an easy way out of his dilemma. The Halloween guerilla squad immediately disbands and reforms as a rescue force. Armed with flu masks and eucalyptus oil, the boys disperse to spread the bad news through the streets of East End, and Brucie follows them blindly. Many hours later, conscience finally sends him to Mah Jim's rescue; but by the time he returns to the privy it is too late for any meaningful action — too late because his friend Mah Li is already dead. The privy had housed Mah Li instead of Mah Jim, and it is this gentle soul who dies like an animal in the midst of his own excrement. And too late because Brucie is already suffering the first symptoms of flu. By the time the boy recovers from his illness, the incident of the privy is a vague memory lost in the larger disaster. Mah Jim is preparing to accompany his brother's corpse back to China, and he interrupts his hasty preparations only to drop off an ironic momento. As the story ends, Brucie is left alone with a tame magpie and the mocking sound of its refrain — "0-5! 0-5!"

Mah Li's death is Brucie's first lesson in the "steady acceptance of consequences" that Stegner admires in Robert Frost and his New England farmers. "I kept thinking how I could have done something when the privy went over and I heard the yell from inside," an older and wiser Bruce remembers; "how I'd had the chance to tell Mr. Menefee and get Mah Li out, but hadn't taken it" (241). Many chances to help and none of them taken. If Brucie had had the courage to stand up for a friend, the tragedy might have been averted. If Brucie had ever acknowledged Mah Li as his friend, his courage might not have been lacking. As a young boy, Brucie cannot articulate all these "if's"; but he is old enough to be aware of his own responsibility and guilt. In "The Chink," Wallace Stegner adds adult understanding to a child's truth of feeling and shows us Mah Li's death for what it was to Brucie — a first step in the painful process of growing up.

In "Saw Gang," published in 1945, we meet another sensitive boy; but this time he is an adolescent, a fifteen-year-old at the threshold of manhood, and actively seeking initiation into the world of adults. Ernie is a child of New England rather than Saskatchewan; thus, he is the inheritor of an infinitely more sophisticated set of values than the crude code of action which molds young Brucie. Moreover, "Saw Gang" is stylistically a very different story from "The Chink." Instead of depending upon a single dramatic incident like Mah Li's death, it proceeds by a gradual but steady process of revelation, a slow illumination of the outlines of Ernie's New England inheritance — virtues, vices, and ambiguities. The psychological development depicted in "Saw Gang" is understated. With strong preconceptions about the nature of work, responsibility, and fellowship, Ernie heads out for a day of labor on a New England work crew. When he returns, nothing remarkable has happened, and none of his notions has really changed. But the existing situation has been intensified — in Stegner's phrase for a Chekhov story — much as bright lights quicken the pace in a darkened theater. And that is enough.

Ernie's day on the saw gang begins early, well before dawn. He is the youngest of this team of rural New Englanders; and, as the work begins, he hangs back for a moment in order to see and copy what the others will do. What they do is set to work, without talking, without choosing a leader, without formally distributing the tasks to be done. And they continue to work, without stopping, without resting, without quarreling over either tasks or tools, until the sun is set. At eleven, a bracing lever hits Will Livesy on the chin; Will laughs, pats his chin in an exploratory way, and without further ado goes back to work. At twelve, there is a brief break for lunch; George Pembroke's wife lays out a spread of meatloaf, potatoes, vegetables, and biscuits, and the team falls to. At three-thirty, John LaPere refills the gas can on his chain saw. These are the only interruptions. Throughout the rest of the long day, Ernie keeps his mouth shut, his back bent, and follows the exhausting example of his fellows. However junior, he is a member of this team, and he offers his best.

Young as he is, Ernie is well aware of the reasons behind his companions' diligence. This is not Mormon country but rural New England, where the self-reliant farmer is the ideal type. A common and compulsive sense of obligation to George Pembroke gets the

saw gang started. It also keeps the gang going long after more comfortable co-workers would have quit. "They would never have
worked like this for any employer," a tired Ernie reflects; "they
kept up the pace only because they all owed George help and would
give nothing but their best day's work in exchange" (75). But this is
an overly simplistic analysis of the gang's motivation; and, in spite
of his exhaustion, Ernie knows it. His teammates are men who
admire competence for its own sake — a competence so self-
confident that it does not even need to call attention to itself. And
they practice competence for its own sake too.

When the saw gang breaks for lunch, the team stops to stare at
the remains of a spruce grove — "whittled and chewed and
mangled with a dull axe and finally broken off instead of being
chopped off clean" (74). Sheepishly, George explains, "That's the
city boy I hired last summer." The men say nothing, whistle and
snort, and move on. There is no need for talk, since all share the
same instinctive response to this conspicuous example of city-bred
bungling. Thus when Will Livesy pauses to let Ernie in on the joke,
and does so with a silent shake of his head, it is an important con-
cession. Throughout the long morning, Ernie has been barred from
full status as a member of the saw gang. Despite his man-sized
labors, the farmers continue to call him "kid" and keep him a distance behind them as they file through the woods. The mangled
spruce stumps present an important augury for the future. Not
now, but sometime in the days to come, they seem to say, Ernie will
prove his competence, earn acceptance, and assume an appropriate
rank within this rural society of peers.

But will Ernie really earn acceptance? And if he does, will he
remain satisfied with it? "Saw Gang" seems confident of an
affirmative answer to these questions; for it is not only the story of
Ernie's successful initiation into a society but a recreation and a
celebration of that society — the simple world of the yeoman
farmer. However, when working in a less nostalgic mood than that
evoked in "Saw Gang," Wallace Stegner is more prepared to
acknowledge the deficiencies of such an insular agrarian environment. For one thing, New England is exclusive and prejudiced in
the patterns of its exclusiveness. In an earlier story called
"Hostage," we meet young Andy Mount, who later reappears in
Stegner's sole New England novel, *Second Growth*. Born and bred
on a New Hampshire farm, Andy is nonetheless branded from

birth as a member of the "no-good" Mount family. Because of this
stigma, it is highly unlikely that labor, however herculean, will ever
earn him a place on the saw gang. Andy learns this lesson as a
youngster. As we shall see in the next chapter, the end of *Second
Growth* finds him leaving his hometown for a larger and more tolerant world.

Moreover, New England is dying, at least as a haven for the yeoman farmer. In a beautiful little story called "The Sweetness of the
Twisted Apples," published in 1948, Stegner juxtaposes a sophisticated young city matron with the tiny wizened figure of a Vermont farm girl who is barely out of her teens but who is "too childish or too prematurely old" (276) for love. The women talk, and
Margaret learns the story of Sary's "disappointment" — a brief,
abortive love affair with the farmer's boy down the road. At first,
Margaret is inclined to pity the girl, to view her whole life as a "disappointment" — frustrated and barren. But this is to judge the girl
in the city's terms when she is properly a part of the autumnal Vermont landscape, with its "wonderful resigned tranquillity" (267) to
its own decay. Like the twisted apples of the old village orchard —
neglected, passed over, but still "sweet, golden, with a strange, wild
tang" (273) — Sary is as serene in the remembrance of her one
"goin' out" as the city girl is in the memory of a lifetime of passionate experience. But Sary's is the serenity of death, not life. All
of Stegner's New England stories are suffused with bittersweet
tenderness for a dying culture. And his New England children —
Ernie, Andy, Sary — all face a special dilemma in their growing up.
They are heirs to a set of values which, if accepted, would prove
limiting but, paradoxically, can be denied only at considerable cost.

In "The Blue-Winged Teal," published in 1950, Stegner observes
a boy like Bruce Mason in the act of cutting himself free from such
a past. Henry Lederer, the story's protagonist, is twenty years old
and a college student. Like Wallace and Bruce before him, Henry
interrupts his studies and returns home to nurse his beloved mother
through her final illness. But unlike his real life and literary forebears, Henry finds himself paralyzed rather than liberated by his
mother's death. Despite the fact that the best of his past dies with
her, Henry lingers at home with the father he hates — temporarily
unable to return to school, look for work, or make contact with the
few hometown friends who share his college experience. The process of "The Blue-Winged Teal" takes Henry to the point where he

overcomes his inertia and moves on to make a new life for himself. In "The Chink," young Brucie comes to terms with friends and friendship, insiders and outsiders alike. In "Saw Gang," Ernie comes to terms with his fellow laborers and the community work ethic made manifest in their activities. But in "The Blue-Winged Teal," Henry comes to terms with the complexities within his own family — the most painful confrontation of all and the most important along the long road to maturity.

John Lederer and his dead wife are the recognizable descendants of George and Hilda Stegner, Bo and Elsa Mason. Details differ, but the critical dichotomies are all there and all the same. John is the prototypical "poolroom-Johnny," handsome in a coarse, "bull-strong" way, the possessor of unexpected and equally useless talents, enchanted by the glamor and extravagance of gambling, but too cautious to take the necessary chances, too sentimental to close his eyes to the necessary human cost. In all, he is a man of many failures, large and small — jobs not taken, friendships not honored, loyalties felt but betrayed. His wife is his natural opposite, perhaps his complement; for she is one of those simple and almost saintly feminine souls that Stegner portrays so well. Both husband and son remember Mrs. Lederer in concrete images of a poignant plainness: lace collars and cuffs scented lightly with sachet and carelessly scattered in a bureau drawer; white china plates carefully hoarded and hand-painted with a single design; and the characteristic affection for the blue-winged teal, not a flashy bird but beautiful in its own way, with a band of bright blue feathers hidden modestly within each wing.

That is all we learn about Mrs. Lederer. But it is enough to allow us to view her, with her husband, in terms of already familiar polarizations — male versus female; father versus mother; vitality, violence, and rugged individualism versus self-sacrifice, compassion, and community. These are the poles that define Henry's experience, the poles that must be brought together in his own life. As the story opens, the boy shows himself to be naive — and, worse, self-destructive — when he seeks to formulate his parents' complex relationship in overly simplistic terms: "she had held the old man up for thirty years, kept him at a respectable job, kept him from slipping back into the poolroom-Johnny he had been when she married him. Within ten days of her death he had hunted up this old failure of a poolhall.... had sprung back into the old pattern, as if his wife had been a jailer and he was now released."[14]

As subsequent developments indicate, Henry must learn to understand and accept his father if he hopes to avoid repetition of the old man's mistakes. For, despite their mutual suspicion and resentment, the two men are much alike; they are locked into similar cycles of guilt, shame, and anger. Henry tries to deny his patrimony, calls his father a callous brute, his mother a martyred misfit, and views his parents' marriage as a thirty-year mistake. Such patent oversimplifications, such evasions of the full complexity of the truth, immobilize their possessor. They maroon Henry in his hometown, accustom him to mindless vegetation. *Tout comprendre c'est tout pardonner,* folk wisdom tells us. Wallace Stegner, an old-fashioned moralist, disagrees and amends the maxim: *Tout comprendre c'est tout comprendre.* That is all. Understanding will never teach Henry to love his father. Old wounds do not heal without leaving a scar. But understanding will liberate the boy from the paralysis born of self-hatred, release him from the chain of childish resentment which binds him to his father, and supply him with the strength to move out on his own.

Understanding bursts upon Henry with the speed and impact of an epiphany — "as if orderly things were breaking and flying apart in his mind" (20). Such nearly mystical moments of growth and illumination — ones in which a protagonist, bright and perceptive but blind in one critical area, suddenly learns to see — provide a particularly satisfying framework for stories of initiation and the discovery of identity. Stegner makes use of these moments throughout his short fiction. "The Chink" and its fellow tales of Saskatchewan boyhood all culminate in a single dramatic revelation. Stories with a contemporary setting revolve around the epiphany experience as well. In the 1946 "Balance His, Swing Yours," for example, a middle-aged Midwesterner momentarily acknowledges his kinship with an ugly, overbearing Englishman, both fellow outcasts at an elegant seaside resort. Similarly, in 1948's "The View from the Balcony," a young warbride pierces through the quiet, civilized facade of a graduate school party and recoils in horrified recognition from the divisiveness, cruelty, and disorder she finds revealed behind it.

Henry Lederer's moment of insight is an equally painful, but more productive, experience. It begins with the boy's return from a successful November duck hunt. As he enters the shabby poolhall, loaded down with a string of fine birds, the regulars receive him as

a mighty huntsman. Several days later, he finds himself the reluctant provisioner for an old-fashioned duck feed — a sordidly sentimental victory feast spread for the benefit of his father's poolroom
cronies. The rich smell of roasting duck mingles with the foul
breath of cigar smoke, cue-chalk dust, and chemical disinfectant.
Max Schmeckebier, the ringleader of the inevitable back-room card
game, mans the stove, while John Lederer forks out huge platefuls
of steaming duck. The orgy of eating and drinking begins, accompanied by crude jokes, satisfied belches, and mawkish reminiscences. Henry views the spectacle with quiet dismay. But when
his father interrupts the feast to salute two graceful teal wings
tacked on the back-bar mirror — an incongruous tribute to his
mother's memory — the boy's dismay becomes silent fury:
"Gabble, gabble, gabble, he said to himself. If you can't think of
anything else to gabble about, gabble about your dead wife. Drag
her through the poolroom too" (19). Henry wants to see his
father's gesture as an act of desecration; but a hasty mirrored
glimpse of pouched eyes and trembling lips, as the old man beats an
awkward retreat from the poolroom, takes the boy abruptly aback.
The bright blue teal wings hold real meaning for John Lederer.
They have moved him to tears.

Viewing his father for the first time with the detached eyes of a
stranger, Henry sees anguish, guilt, and the consciousness of failure
inscribed on his aging face. Suddenly, the old man's veneer of
geniality and good spirits is pitifully easy to penetrate. His sporting
life is an evasion; his whores and crap games, cheap tickets to obliv-
ion; and the sordid mechanics of the pool hall, one of "the careful
games that deadened you into sleep" (21). John Lederer deserves
his son's sympathy more than his hatred; and, in the end, oddly
enough, he receives his just deserts. When Henry understands his
past and accepts it, in full comprehension of its continuity with the
present, he is free to depart, and does so. But his departure is no
victory. As Stegner describes it, in a moving final image, Henry
bids his father farewell "with the feeling he might have had on
letting go the hand of a friend too weak and too exhausted to cling
any longer to their inadequate shared driftwood in a wide cold sea"
(22). Tolerance, sympathy, the ability to see through another's eyes:
little Brucie has come a long way from East End.

IV *Joe*

In 1946, four years before the appearance of "The Blue-Winged Teal," Wallace Stegner published a very good short story called "The Women on the Wall." It failed to excite much critical interest at the time; and it did not attract one of the prestigious prizes that were fast becoming standard fare for Stegner. But it has remained throughout the years one of its author's favorites — and with good reason, for it was a prophetic piece, prophetic of Stegner's future course as a writer of short fiction. By 1946, Wallace had arrived at Stanford, critical success, and the not very advanced age of thirty-seven. Although he would continue to write in the "Brucie" mode for several more years, the saga of the sensitive adolescent must already have begun to lose interest for him. Boyhood memories were fast fading; both of his parents were dead; the peculiar problems of the intellectual outlander had been long surmounted. And, despite occasional exceptions, the best of the "Brucie" stories were also in his past, back with the sense of unfulfilled aspiration that dominates *The Big Rock Candy Mountain*. Recognition of this sort must have been in Stegner's mind as he sat down to write "The Women on the Wall," for, as a short story, it is a real departure from his previous work. It is an attempt to create a contemporary setting and deal with contemporary problems — a sure-footed step away from the familiar terrain of Whitemud, Greensboro, Salt Lake, and Iowa Cities.

The story deals with the changing perceptions of an elderly colonial who has been ejected from a comfortable post on the Galapagos by the turbulence of World War II and has resettled on a quiet stretch of California coastline. Mr. Palmer spends his mornings in an airy study overlooking the ocean, ostensibly engaged in reordering his memoirs. But, in fact, he is often content just to gaze from his windows, survey the rolling Pacific, and immerse himself in the activities of a bevy of military wives who occupy a nearby row of beachfront apartments. There are six major figures in this group, and Mr. Palmer soon learns to recognize them all: placid Mrs. Kendall and her quiet little son; vivacious Mrs. Corson and her quick-footed daughter; boyish Margy Fisher in the inevitable bathing suit and bare feet; and slow-moving Hope Vaughn, six months pregnant.

Mr. Palmer enjoys watching all the group's comings and goings, but he is especially delighted with the daily ritual of the morning mail. From his window, the women look like figures in an ancient Greek frieze as they gather each day on the low stone wall facing the letter boxes and wait, pricked out by the clear California sunshine, for the regular arrival and departure of the old gray mail car. The letters control their fates in a very direct way, bringing messages of life and death from soldier husbands. For the women, this waiting is a significant activity: indeed, their wartime mission appears to be a passive but important one — preserving ancient patterns of nurturance and continuity in the midst of a disorderly world. Old Mr. Palmer idealizes the women as modern Penelopes, admires their patience and fidelity, and resolves to leave them undisturbed in their waiting. He decides that they will not benefit from the intrusion of his pity. Penelope, he recalls with satisfaction, was as competent for her waiting as Ulysses was for his wars and his wiles.

Had Mr. Palmer kept to his scholar's eyrie, his insights might have culminated in this classical parallel; the story might have ended with women, children, sea, and sun caught in a kind of symbolic stasis. But, being human, the old gentleman breaks his resolve, leaves his perch, and edges closer and closer to the women on the wall and to the real lives hidden behind their waiting. The first hint of discord comes with the death of Captain Fisher; for, as far as Mr. Palmer can see, there is no group support for his bereaved wife, no communal keening for the lost hero. Overnight, the thin, barefoot widow simply vanishes from her accustomed place on the wall. A second hint comes with the appearance and disappearance of a half-grown cocker pup. A pet for Tommy Kendall, the pup spends two lonely days tied to the end of a rose trellis, barking and whining and begging for his freedom. Finally, Mrs. Corson puts an end to the general misery with a quick call to the Society for the Prevention of Cruelty to Animals. Relieved at the dog's departure, Mr. Palmer steps out of his study long enough to commiserate with Mrs. Corson. Soon, and not entirely to his displeasure, he finds himself corralled into accompanying her and her daughter on a shopping excursion.

Having arrived downtown, Mr. Palmer readily agrees to treat young Anne to a pony ride while her mother runs errands. Time passes, one pony ride stretches to two, three, four, and five, and the old gentleman gradually grows perturbed. At last, Mrs. Corson returns and drives the trio back home to the beach, but she brings increased cause for agitation along with her. Her eyes are dilated, her

manner frenetic, her sharp tongue quick as a cat's. Leaving Mr.
Palmer no opportunity to protest, she bursts into an animated and
vicious recitation of her group's carefully guarded secrets. Tommy
Kendall is adopted, his mother an overprotective prude; Hope
Vaughn is pregnant with a stranger's child. On top of it all, Mrs.
Corson has a secret of her own; she is addicted to pep pills and pot,
which she procures at the local fortune-teller's.

Desperately, unsuccessfully, Mr. Palmer tries to contain Mrs.
Corson's tidal wave of words. Neighbors are staring, children
eavesdropping, and Mrs. Kendall has dissolved in tears. At last, a
literal *deus ex machina,* the mail car arrives on its daily round. As if
by magic, the recriminations cease. Mrs. Corson, Mrs. Kendall,
and Mrs. Vaughn assume their regular places by the low stone wall
and wait patiently in the Attic sunlight for the ritual of distribution,
reading, and relief to unfold. The story ends abruptly, much as it
begins, with a colorful pageant spread out before Mr. Palmer, and
speculation as to its meaning revolving in his mind. Viewed at close
range, as individuals, the waiting women lose their simplified, symbolic stasis and are revealed to him as fellow mortals; frustrated,
violent, they are at war with one another and with their common
fate. The peaceful resignation he has imagined in them is no more
than grudging submission to the empty monotony of their lives.

As an elderly colonial, well-educated and well-traveled, retired
from work, without family or an active role in life, Mr. Palmer is a
very different character from Bruce Mason. Indeed, he seems to
represent a dramatic departure from the "personal heresy" prom-
ulgated in *The Writer in America* — the firm foundation in deeply
felt personal experience that Stegner has hitherto seen as the necessary prerequisite for building believable fiction. How to explain the
story's success in light of these contradictions? Fortunately for the
student, Stegner resolves them for us in "A Problem in Fiction," a
detailed recreation of the gestative process which gave birth to
"The Women on the Wall."[15]

According to its author, the story did originate in personal experience, but it was personal experience of a relatively abstract kind
— an internal confrontation with the validity of symbol making.
Like old Mr. Palmer, Wallace Stegner spent a series of stolen mornings spying on the daily ritual of a group of military wives. And,
like his elderly alter-ego, he first viewed the women symbolically, as
the essence of fecund quiescence and cyclical growth; later, with the

addition of a classical parallel, he perceived them as the contemporary equivalents of faithful Penelope. As an artist, Stegner's next task was to set his characters in motion, to devise a meaningful plot for the women to act out. But, when he tried to do so, he failed; and his failure helped him recognize the falsity of his original conception. His symbols and parallels were pure imposition. They told him more about himself than they did about the women, who were doubtless as confused and angry as anybody else underneath the placid surface of their daily routine. In short, if Stegner had a story, it was a story about himself and his own growth in sympathy and understanding. Better yet, it was a story about a man very much like himself, but not himself, whom he could observe with the detachment and irony appropriate to fiction.

Hence, Mr. Palmer, a rather conservative old gentleman, scholarly in his interests, analytical in his approach to life, but earnest, even sentimental, a lover of animals and children, and an irrepressible knight-errant in the face of feminine distress. With his creation in 1946, Stegner had happened upon the voice, the persona, that was to serve him best in his middle years. Details differ, but the general features of Mr. Palmer's personality recur constantly in the major male characters of Stegner's subsequent short fiction, permitting him to explore the perennial problems of familial and communal identity long after their permanent resolution in his own life, and providing him with the perfect solution for a persistent technical problem as well.

As we have noted, an imperfect control of the varieties of point of view is the greatest weakness in Stegner's early fiction. In his early tales, no doubt because of their deeply felt autobiographical basis, he tends to allow the perspectives of protagonist and author to merge. At key moments, for example, Bruce Mason and his creator are almost indistinguishable. Of course, this identification of author and protagonist has its advantages. "The Chink," "Saw Gang," and "The Blue-Winged Teal" are all strengthened by the unusual degree of enlightened self-scrutiny that their heroes bring to bear on the business of growing up. But identification of this kind deprives Stegner of some of the most potent weapons in the literary arsenal, most notably irony; it also seems to result in occasional overwriting. Subtly suggestive stories like "The Sweetness of the Twisted Apples" and "The Blue-Winged Teal" are marred by the insertion of superfluous soliloquies and by unnecessarily explicit psychological summaries. According to Robert Frost, the writer deserves credit for whatever the reader gets. Whatever the explanation — perhaps he is too personally involved in his material, perhaps he is as yet unsure of his powers of dramatization — the early Stegner too frequently cuts himself off from the full range of risks and advantages suggested by Frost's critical precept.

In "The Women on the Wall," we are spectators to the emergence of a perfect vehicle for Stegner's mature speculations about the business of growing up. As a small "d" democrat, Stegner is a firm believer in old-fashioned institutions such as work, marriage, and the family. Nonetheless, he is also fully aware of the fragility and intermittent failure of these institutions, as well as the impossibility of doing more than merely suggesting their value to anybody else. Such things, he believes, the young must learn for themselves.

Not altogether unlike his maker, Mr. Palmer is a convincing spokesman for the classical Protestant virtues; on the other hand, he is naive, idiosyncratic, and somewhat out-of-date. Despite his growth in understanding, the old man never manages to provide any real support for the women on the wall. His insights, authentic but completely internalized, are of value to no one but himself. We know that Stegner sympathizes with elements of Palmer's point of view; but, at the same time, we are made aware of its impotence. Such subtle distinctions would be impossible without the measure of authorial detachment increasingly evident in Stegner's later work.

One of Mr. Palmer's more notable descendants appears in "The Traveler," a story published in 1951. A middle-aged drug salesman happens upon the reincarnation of his childhood self — an imaginative young orphan, isolated on his grandparents' back country farm, and hungry for the stimulation and excitement of the outside world. The traveler is exhilarated by this unexpected return to his past, and moves on refreshed and strengthened in his sense of himself. But despite this, and despite the fact that he is a peddler of "miracle" drugs, he finds himself unable to minister to the boy's needs, unable to reassure him that he will find a more rewarding world. For that "most chronic and incurable of ills, identity" (206), each man must act as his own physician. Similarly, in "Impasse," published two years later, a father learns to live with insights he cannot and would not share, even if he could. His difficult only daughter is not a pretty girl. Hitherto, her rebelliousness has seemed like ingratitude; now, it is revealed to him as the pathetic product of youthful illusion. Once free of her parents' effusive care, Margaret hopes to excite the attention and romantic admiration so far denied her because of physical disadvantages. Just as she is doomed to discover her self-deception, so her father must stand helplessly by as the dreary drama unfolds itself.

Like Mr. Palmer, Margaret's father and the medical salesman experience impotence, but they do so without arousing in their readers the strong feelings of pity and apprehension inspired by "The Women on the Wall." As characters, they are relatively thin and underdeveloped; they cannot sustain Mr. Palmer's burden of imprisoned insight. Indeed, "The Traveler" and "Impasse" attract our attention chiefly as literary way stations; they are tales which employ the elderly observer figure introduced in "The Women on the Wall," experimenting with him, keeping him alive through the late 1940s and early 1950s while Stegner brings the saga of Bruce Mason to a conclusion. At the end of the journey are "Field Guide to the Western Birds," a splendid novella published in 1956, and Joe Allston, the cantankerous ex-literary agent who narrates the story. Allston is not Wallace Stegner; rather, he is Mr. Palmer perfected. He is a Westerner, but a recent and somewhat reluctant arrival on the West Coast. His best years have been spent in New York, and he brings an arrogant outsider's eye to bear on the easy platitudes of Western life. On the other hand, he has had ample opportunity to observe the foibles of the Eastern literary establishment. Intelligent, opinionated to the point of prejudice, but at the same time acutely aware of his own limitations, Joe is constantly assessing the facts and fictions in his own attitudes and experience. He combines within himself strong personal prepossessions and fierce self-scrutiny. As such, he is an ideal guide to "the middle ground."

"Field Guide" describes Joe's experience at a chic Northern California cocktail party *cum* musicale. His hosts, the Casements, are fantastically, almost preternaturally wealthy folk who are also friendly, self-effacing, with that endearing innocence occasionally characteristic of the very rich. Sue Casement is the party's presiding genius. Like most of Stegner's Western women, pioneer or contemporary, she is a humble worshipper at the shrine of culture, an irrepressible protectress of neglected artists. Her musical extravaganza is a good-natured plot to promote the career of her latest protege,

Arnold Kaminski, pianist from Poland, an unrecognized refugee genius. Kaminski plays well and impresses his elegant, handpicked audience. His arrogance is egregious but acceptable, part of the price people like the Casements expect to pay for participation in the great world of art. But after the departure of most of the guests, Kaminski gets drunk and oversteps even the generous rules of artistic license. Deliberately, gratuitously, inexplicably, he insults his ingenuous hostess and nips his own burgeoning career in the bud.

Joe Allston, always the last guest to leave, surveys the developing crisis with wonder. He has spent his time at the cocktail party identifying and observing the entire spectrum of "western birds": fashionable San Francisco aesthetes, beagle-breeders from the Hillsborough horsey set, and miscellaneous, mesmerized hangers-on. In its own way, Joe's undertaking is as arrogant and unproductive as Kaminski's; for, in spite of his confidence, he fails to classify the guests or to predict their behavior. He returns home to his imperfect hillside a much chastened man, perturbed and unsettled by his somewhat voyeuristic research into the complexities of human intercourse. In his own irreverent dialect, he is a bird watcher brought down to the level of the birds.

Even this brief summary should be sufficient to suggest the technical excellence of "Field Guide." To begin with, let us admire Stegner's superb resolution of the problem of point of view. This is the first story since "The Chink" to be written in the first person, and the advantages Stegner realizes in his use of the device are decisive for his future work. "Field Guide" may be viewed as the structural model for *All the Little Live Things* and *Angle of Repose,* two of Stegner's most successful novels. Joe Allston provides the reader with a plausible, consistent, and informative perspective from which to observe the Casement extravaganza. Certainly not omniscient, limited and often erroneous in its insights, invariably controversial, but always interesting for its own sake, his line of vision is occasionally outrageously funny and never dull. At the same time, Allston provides Stegner with what must have seemed like the irresistible opportunity to satirize gently a familiar type, the literary agent — not a writer, but a writer's wet nurse. Allston's mode of discourse is a curious mixture of the acute and the inappropriate. Stegner organizes his narrator's thoughts and words in a manner that approaches stream of consciousness, juxtaposing colloquialism and classicism, telling detail and injudicious generalization, just as they occur in the most private recesses of Allston's mind. The process culminates in a daring mock-Vergilian description of Kaminski's performance of a Bach chaconne: "As when in the San Francisco Cow Palace, loudspeakers announce the draft horse competition, and sixteen great Percherons trot with high action and ponderous foot into the arena, brass-harnessed, plume-bridled, swelling with power, drawing the rumbling brewery wagon lightly, Regal Pale . . ." (163–64). An outrageous comparison for one of the master works of classical music? Of course, but one entirely consistent with the compulsive irreverence characteristic of Joe Allston.

At the beginning of this chapter we outlined Wallace Stegner's critical position, highlighting his conviction that the writer must impose form upon experience without loss of truth. As a narrator, Joe Allston provides an especially effective way of meeting this artistic obligation. Joe's distinctively analytical approach to life reduces the chaos of the Casement cocktail party to a readily assimilable order. He isolates the important guests, describes them in detail, and records the significant moments in their conversation. Naturally, this process falsifies as it simplifies; if Sue Casement or Arnold Kaminski were our narrators, they would doubtless make entirely different selections. But the "truth" lost in terms of the entire party experience is neatly counterbalanced by the "truth" gained in terms of Joe Allston's personality. This is a compromise to be sure, but a pretty good one. If we learn very little about the genus of California party-goers, we learn a great deal about a more interesting species, the retired literary agent.

"Field Guide" is also remarkable for its convincing evocation of place and for its skillful use of natural, especially animal imagery. True, we have paused over Stegner's impressive descriptive powers before; but, with the exception of the New England stories, his descriptions have rarely ventured beyond the boundaries of the Stegner country. At their best, they have been renderings of virgin Western landscape, the less populous the better, such as the majestic river canyons that blocked exploration beyond the hundredth meridian. More cluttered with humans, a California cocktail party demands a response more complex in its mingling of sentiments. Yet Stegner, through Joe, succeeds in portraying the party in sharp yet subtly telling colors. His recreation of the "Casement Club" — "chaste and hypnotically comfortable and faintly oppressive with money, like an ad for one of the places where you will find *News-*

week" (135), and his lovingly Lucullan catalog of the party refresh-
ments — "trenchers as big as cafeteria trays," "a state fair exhibit
of salads," and "a marvelous molded crab with pimento eyes
afloat in a tidepool of mayonnaise" (150), fairly catch the tone.

Cheek by jowl with such graphic culinary detail we find a host of
ambiguous metaphors drawn from the animal kingdom. Impulsive
Joe is seen as a feisty little terrier; his gently assertive wife Ruth as a
pert, ironical raccoon. In addition, Joe pursues his original "bird
watching" conceit as relentlessly as any of his classical allusions.
Kaminski appears as a homeless cuckoo chick, while his unlucky
hosts, the Casements, play the role of a pair of reluctantly adoptive
robins. And "Field Guide" opens and closes with the image of a
towhee locked in prolonged combat with his reflection in a plate
glass window. This odd menagerie of creatures suggests an attitude
toward our animal inheritance that is neither encomiastic nor
abusive, but simply accepting. Nature, even human nature, is
essentially self-absorbed and indifferent to moral distinctions; both
present a *tabula rasa* to the complex network of artificial constraints that we call civilization. In short, "Field Guide" debunks
the romantic myth of nature's infinite bounty as surely as historical
and biographical works such as *Beyond the Hundredth Meridian*
do, and it does so in the more pliant fictional form that we have
called Stegner's "middle ground."

Idealization of nature's bounty is one tenet of the romantic faith;
virtual idolatry of nature's human mimic, the creative artist, is
another. A born iconoclast, Joe Allston delights in the deflation of
both myths; but in "Field Guide" it is the latter that absorbs his
attention, excites his wrath, and provides the fulcrum that sets this
doubly ironic drama into motion. The minute Joe enters the Casement Club he recognizes Kaminski for a "Glandular Genius" (142)
— familiarly known as the "G.G." (143). This is a type Joe has
come to know and despise during his long years as a literary agent.
A "G.G." is an artist who thinks himself cut from a finer cloth
than ordinary mortals, who believes that his special abilities render
him less rather than more responsible for fulfilling the obligations
incurred in everyday life. Kaminski is selfish, oversensitive,
affected, and self-pitying, eager for emotional self-indulgence of
every kind. In Joe's eyes, he displays all the stigmata of the
Glandular Genius and displays them with a sense of pride.

Allston, on the other hand, sees himself as a "defender, self-

appointed, of the good American middle class small-town and suburban way of life'' (170). *All the Little Live Things* tells us that Joe
is a transplanted Midwesterner, but his heritage is clearly implied in
"Field Guide," for he is burdened with all the built-in ambivalences that gave birth to DeVoto's *The Literary Fallacy.* Joe reveres
literature but rejects the contemporary literary life-style; he
admires Byron but condemns Byronic posturing. Unlike Kaminski,
he associates cultural achievement with self-control, with the cooperative spirit, and with a healthy respect for traditional institutions. In short, his values are those which Hilda Stegner, who knew
what life was like without them, saw as the foundation of
civilization.

As we know, these values are also Wallace Stegner's; indeed, the
Stegner biography outlined in Chapter 1 is testimony to the fact
that the creative life can be as orderly as it is inventive. But, as we
have taken pains to point out, "Field Guide" is fiction rather than
autobiography; and Joe Allston, while a sympathetic character, is
one his creator can view with detachment. The Casement cocktail
party would scarcely serve as an interesting subject for a story if it
left Joe's prepossessions exactly as it found them. Intensification is
sufficient justification for a very short piece such as "Saw Gang,"
but we look for growth and development in a novella of nearly
seventy pages, and we get it. "Field Guide" is successful because it
makes use of a double, reverberant pattern of psychological re-
versal. It confirms Joe's insights, but it also undercuts them. In
doing so, it suggests the limitations of human understanding, the
imperfectness of the growing up process which we have been
tracing throughout Stegner's short fiction.

Allston is right to despise the Glandular Genius but wrong to see
Kaminski as a clear-cut representative of that pernicious class.
Like most people, Kaminski is complex enough to defy categoriza-
tion. He is too talented to need to play the "G.G.," yet too self-
destructive to play the role right. He is both criminal and accuser,
victim and victimizer. Whatever his deficiencies, he deserves
Allston's compassion much more than his contempt. As soon as
Allston becomes aware of this, the texture of his discourse abruptly
changes. Hitherto, "Field Guide" has been rigorously naturalistic;
now the natural gives way to the surreal. The closing moments of
the Casement party read like the final frames of a Marx brothers
comedy. Kaminski makes indecent remarks to a homely little music

teacher. He dodges his hostess' enraged husband, throws chairs, and falls flat on his face into a darkened swimming pool. In the end, he has to be fished out of three feet of water as unceremoniously as a drowned rat.

Joe Allston finds himself less and less able to identify the villain of this melodrama. As he drives home in the encroaching Peninsula fog — the perfect physical reflection for his inner feelings of moral uncertainty — he asks himself the ultimate, unanswerable questions. What kind of person is this Kaminski? Where does he fit in? Even if he is the human anomaly he appears to be, does not society have a place for him, a use for his peculiar talents? Or will the time-honored institutions that sustain other people always work against him, betray him, exclude him, confirm the fact that he does not belong? Despite Joe's eccentricities, he is a thoughtful man, and his experiences in "Field Guide" work to refine a maturity that is already remarkable. Like Andy Mount, Henry Lederer, and Bruce Mason, Joe has come to terms with his own friends and family. His life has been one steady affirmation of traditional values — hard work, marital fidelity, a well-earned and honorable retirement. But like Mr. Palmer, Joe has also come to terms with the dark side of the traditional life style. Age-old patterns provide continuity, security, order, control; but they cannot provide all things for all people. Motherhood does not help the women on the wall any more than mothering helps Arnold Kaminski. In sum, maturity means resignation as well as reconciliation. As Joe Allston puts it at the end of "Field Guide," "I don't know whether I'm tired, or sad, or confused. Or maybe just irritated that they don't give you enough time in a single life to figure anything out" (194).

CHAPTER 4

Remembering Laughter *to*
The Preacher and The Slave

I *Points of Departure*

IT is a familiar axiom of Aristotelian philosophy that a wise man never attempts to exceed the limits of precision that his particular discipline allows. The mathematician, for example, is within reach of a more highly precise but narrower variety of truth than, say, the psychologist. Joe Allston's frustration at the close of "Field Guide" is a reluctant but faithfully Aristotelian admission that life is a terribly complex and random affair and that the precise formulation of its meaning (or meanings) is virtually impossible. In order to achieve wisdom in the science of life, Joe seems to say, one must admit that questions about human motive and human desire cannot be answered with much accuracy. The "what" of behavior is fairly straightforward: Joe goes to a party, sees certain people, and does certain things. "Why" he goes to the party, "why" he sees certain people and not others, and "why" he performs certain actions are questions likely to make Aristotelians of all but the most myopic observers of the human scene.

Joe's frustration is the mark of his wisdom, for he knows what he cannot know about behavior. The fact that his declaration of skepticism appears at the conclusion of an action that he has narrated is peculiarly resonant. Joe acknowledges what all storytellers — historians included — must acknowledge, that while we can record the details of human activity with remarkable precision, we must proceed with caution and humility when we address ourselves to the psychological phenomena behind such activity. All of which brings us back to the concept of "the middle ground."

Taking Wallace Stegner's cue, we have defined "the middle ground" as the dramatic rendering of historical persons, places, and events. The terrain is extensive enough to accommodate both historians and writers of fiction, and — for Stegner at least — the persons, places, and events involved are usually Western. We have added, drawing on the essay "History, Myth, and the Western Writer," that an author achieves "the middle ground" to the degree that he is able to discover and articulate continuities between past and present. It is Faulkner's great contribution that he has done this for the South. But who, Stegner wonders, will do it for the West? Who will make the Western past usable by linking it to the Western present? The question is more than slightly disingenuous, but all is forgiven when Stegner admits that he would like to be the dramatist of continuities beyond the hundredth meridian.

A warning. "The middle ground" is not a neutral concept; it is a set of values relating to the business of history and literature. As such, it does not exhaust the potential of either area, nor can it pretend to enunciate the final or even the most desirable goals for historians and "creative" writers. Granted, many historians have concerned themselves with cultural continuities. Others have turned their attention to very specific and local events, or to historical matters such as revolution, which are treated as special, relatively isolated problems. A few historians would argue that the only continuities are the ones their more optimistic colleagues invent. In the same vein, many novels and short stories contain historical material, and it is probably true that all fictions have some social, and therefore historical, significance. But such significance is no more an absolute value in literature than the discovery of continuities is in history. In other words, "the middle ground" is only one among many important sets of historical and literary standards. Since Stegner has declared himself in pursuit of "the middle ground," it is only just that he be reckoned with in the light of his own very reasonable goals. On the other hand, he would no doubt agree that there are other perfectly reasonable historical and literary ideals that have little direct bearing on his own work.

To this point we have observed Stegner's progress toward "the middle ground" in history and in the short story. Success as an historian, most notably in *Beyond the Hundredth Meridian,* has been the result of evident enthusiasm tempered by detachment. Powell's heroism is perfectly plausible, even in the context of prominent, less heroic, Western continuities. It boils down to point of view. In the biography, Stegner's esteem for Powell strikes us as just; the picture is balanced; the facts bear him out. The same cannot be said for *Mormon Country*. In that very early book, authorial prejudice expresses itself in the omission of some facts and in the distorted interpretation of others. As an historian, then, Stegner has come closest to "the middle ground" when his point of view has intruded least, or when its intrusion has not led to misrepresentation.

It is more difficult to generalize about the short fiction, since most of the stories are too brief to be described as dramatic renderings of historical continuities. It follows that few of them qualify as examples of "the middle ground." We can discuss them in the same context as the historical nonfiction, however, if we consider the problem of the author's prepossessions about his material. Initially, we venture the opinion that Stegner is least successful with the omniscient point of view. The problem is symptomatic: he has strong prepossessions about his characters, and too often his voice is audible behind the thin veil of objectivity. He is much more successful with an involved narrator such as Joe Allston, who speaks in the first person. Again, explanations come readily to mind. There is no premium on the illusion of neutrality in stories told from a character's point of view, or in a character's voice. To the contrary, we no more anticipate neutrality in fictional characters than we do in real ones. For good reasons, however, we expect it from the best storytellers, just as we expect it from the best historians. Given this much, Joe Allston is an ideal solution to the problem of point of view in Stegner's short fiction: he is extremely opinionated, but his opinions are his own. It matters not at all that many of Joe's convictions — on the Glandular Genius, for example — are the prized possessions of his creator. To the degree that he disguises his own voice in his stories, Wallace Stegner approaches that illusion of authorial detachment which is the essential first step toward "the middle ground."

Further steps take place in the novels, where there is room for the development of historical themes. We will return to this question in the sections that follow. For the moment, a word on our organization of the long fiction may be in order. In the thirty-six years since 1937, Wallace Stegner has published ten novels. Some of them have been written quickly, in a matter of weeks; others have occupied several years. A few are very long, though most are relatively short. With one exception, all of the novels are set in the West. About half of them are historical novels. Most of the rest include historical sections or make reference to a past which influences the present. They vary in quality almost as much as they vary in length.

There were clear alternatives to the chronological approach that we have taken. Several of the novels are dominated by women. Had we discussed these books in separation from the rest of the canon, no doubt rich perspectives on Stegner's attitudes to women would have been the result. We might have divided the novels into those that treat young people and those that treat adults, or we might have divided them by theme. There are good arguments for separating the novels that deal with the past from those that deal with the present. We have opted for strict chronology because we are inclined to view Stegner's long fiction as a developing unity. His main themes — we have touched on most of them in preceding chapters — are remarkably persistent. His technical development has been irregular, but, in general, practice has meant movement toward perfection. Most crucially, the novels strike us as the record of Stegner's struggle with the problem of point of view. If he has solved the problem — and we feel that he has — then we will do best to review the struggle in its consecutive stages.

II   *Getting Started*

Remembering Laughter, published in 1937, marks Wallace Stegner's arrival on the American literary scene. Completed in about six weeks, the novelette won the Little, Brown prize, and earned warm praise from the critics. Viewed in retrospect, *Remembering Laughter* displays several characteristics which were to become standard fare in Stegner's novels. The setting is rural Iowa, an important margin of the Stegner country. From the outset the reader is impressed with the author's intimate familiarity with the regional landscape and with the routines of farm life. The action occurs in the past, during the first two decades of the present century. Of the three principal characters, two are women. The story develops from their point of view. The plot is a fictionalized adaptation of family history — in this case, the family was Mary Stegner's, though the characters were types well known to her husband. More than a good start, the novelette was an augury of greater things to come.

The story begins with what we later recognize as an ending. Margaret Stuart, whose "face was parchment over bone,"[1] appears much older than her forty-seven years. Seated motionless in a rocker, she stares impassively through the parlor window at the guests arriving for her husband's funeral. Elspeth, her sister, enters the dark silence of the room. Though seven years younger than Margaret, Elspeth "looked like her twin. The same tightly drawn hair, the same high forehead and sharp nose with the nostrils bitten in, the same cavernous eye-sockets and ice-blue eyes, the same raw-boned, gaunt, poplin-clad figure" (6). They speak in short, hushed fragments. The words have a soft Scotch burr about them. It is time for the funeral to begin. The guests are waiting. Malcolm is in his room grieving. When their eyes meet, the sisters exchange a look neither hostile nor cold: "There was something in it that struggled toward warmth, as if sympathy and affection were fighting to the surface through crusted years of repression and control" (7).

This very brief, enigmatic prologue raises more questions than it answers. Two prematurely aged Scottish sisters bend under the burden of a bitter but unexplained past. If there is a hint of affection between them, there is something darker as well. They speak haltingly, as if in terror of their emotions; and we wonder why. Do these feelings have something to do with the funeral of Alec Stuart, Margaret's husband? How did he die? And who is Malcolm? In their minds, the sisters dwell on the memory of a day eighteen years in the past: "the lips of the woman in the chair were twisted with the bitterness of it" (8). Vaguely suggestive, an intimation of grim catastrophe, the subtle suspense of the prologue puts the reader on the edge of his chair.

Questions quickly give way to answers. The first chapter takes us back eighteen years. Alec Stuart, a prosperous farmer and land-owner, stands with his pretty wife, Margaret, on the platform of the Spring Mills station. With the train comes Elspeth, who has traveled from Scotland to live with them. She is as pretty as her sister, but fuller of life and animal energy. Alec, who feels that his wife's disgust with drink is a little extreme, is taken immediately with Elspeth's fresh, wide-eyed innocence. He regales her with tall Western tales as they drive back to the farm. The contrast between the sisters is quite evident. Margaret is very formal, a trifle haughty, prim, proper, in all a starched Scottish Calvinist. Elspeth is curious, enthusiastic, excitable, a bit of a rogue. We encounter Margaret indoors, in the kitchen, or in the company parlor, a room which her sister finds "painfully clean, so formal and unliveable"

(22). Elspeth is forever outdoors, feeding chickens, taking walks with Alec, exploring the barn, chatting with Ahlquist, the powerful, blond hired man. Characteristically, Margaret warns her away. Ahlquist is a married man; his family is in Norway, awaiting his return; he is below Elspeth's station; there is the risk of gossip. She speaks with "stiff puritan disapproval behind her words" (31). Elspeth fails to understand, but she sees less of Ahlquist.

Imagining her sister lonely, Margaret plans a party. Her intentions could not be more obvious. The minister, the doctor, the sons of a local English gentleman — the guests are a collection of well-washed, eligible, utterly boring bachelors. After supper there is singing, dancing, followed by a controversial round of "Post Office." The Reverend Hitchcock disapproves, as does Margaret, who grows increasingly waspish. Meanwhile Alec — irritated with his wife's stiffness, half-conscious of what has become his passion for Elspeth, and jealous of the fumbling suitors — withdraws to the barn with some cronies for a drink. Later on, when Elspeth retrieves him, she offers little resistance to his embrace. Suddenly they share a terrible secret.

"When Elspeth awoke next morning that moment in the shadow of the barn was like something she had dreamed" (68). Confused, ashamed, overcome with fear, Elspeth resolves to avoid further intimacy with Alec. At their first meeting, however, she discovers the extent of her weakness in the presence of his frank virility and her own desire. Sterner resolutions follow. She avoids Alec whenever possible. In his presence she defends herself with strained jocularity. Smoldering, Alec waits. Before long circumstance and the inevitability of their desire combine to make them lovers. For a brief time shame is balanced with passion in a series of secret meetings. When Margaret finally discovers them, Elspeth begins to realize, more fully and painfully than she could have imagined, that deeds have consequences.

Discovery of betrayal and infidelity sets off a chain of powerful reactions in Margaret. She retires to her bedroom to wait for Alec, to hope — against hope — that he will not come, and to let her thoughts settle. At first she is overcome with jealousy. Gradually a veil of religious rationalization spreads through her mind, softening her wrath into pious indignation. The sad resignation that follows is brief and imperfect: "By slow degrees Margaret's jealousy was transformed and masked, but the progress toward resignation was broken by paroxysms of rebellious fury, and the image that filled her mind was not of the lost souls before the tribunal of a just God, but of two shadows fumbling for the ladder to the loft'' (95).

When Margaret finally emerges from her room, she is apparently calm, her passionate resentment contained. She presents a cool, courteous, but distant exterior. Elspeth is meek-eyed, submissive, her vitality buried forever in guilt and remorse. Alec's submission expresses itself in withdrawal; he looks after the farm. What Margaret cannot forget, she can control; and the revelation that Elspeth is pregnant does little to upset her apparent self-possession. She controls the situation by giving Ahlquist enough money to return to Norway. The town, she realizes, will know what to make of his hasty, unexplained disappearance. The child, Malcolm, grows up believing that Margaret and Elspeth — cold, remote, humorless women — are his aunts. His "uncle" is the sole source of joy and pleasure in the boy's life. Alec possesses a surplus of vitality; when he is alone with Malcolm, there is time and spirit for tall tales and a bellylaugh. He remembers laughter and gives it to his son.

This dark, enigmatic tale closes with Malcolm's emergence into early manhood and with Alec's sudden death. An epilogue brings us back to the funeral that was about to get under way in the prologue. When the mourners have departed, Malcolm confronts the pale sisters; he challenges them to acknowledge that Elspeth is his mother, Alec his father. Their stunned silence is admission enough. With a promise that he will write each week and with money from his father's estate, he leaves. He will return, we have no doubt, but not until he has adjusted to the burden of his new knowledge. The conflict between Margaret and Elspeth dies with Alec. They are reconciled, though their consolations are slender ones: "As surely as they knew that they were sisters again, they knew that they were old women. Eighteen years of sunless living lay upon them like a blight, and with Malcolm had gone their last hold upon that life which still knew laughter and a light heart" (153).

In hands less skillful than Stegner's, *Remembering Laughter* might have become implausible melodrama. The plot is a little too neat; crucial episodes hinge on improbable coincidence. Stegner avoids what is potentially awkward in the story by converting weaknesses to strengths. In matters of tone, pace, and style, he moves away from strict, highly detailed realism toward a compact and symbolic manner that approaches parable or myth. The narrative is brief; the episodes are few, though they combine to form a tight, rather straightforward thematic unity. There is little that could be called "background" in the piece. What happened before Elspeth arrived, or what will happen after Malcolm's departure, are left to the reader's imagination. We have a definite sense of place, but that effect is achieved with a few deft, economical strokes. The secondary characters are flat, sketchy types; they are not allowed to distract us from the three characters at the center of the action. The prologue and epilogue constitute a kind of frame, and they work to intensify our impression of a dominant foreground.

Such deliberate limitations of time and space and action and character create a slightly unreal atmosphere. Intensification issues from simplification. The compression is artful in the best sense. This is a compact microcosm in which all gestures, all actions, all utterances, bear heightened significance. Style augments this impression. Comparing Margaret and Alec in their youth, Stegner writes, "She was tall, but not so tall as he, and she was slender, and the bloom still on her" (9). Repetition, accentuated rhythms, delicate colloquialism, scarce but poignant detail — the prose is slightly elevated toward the poetic, and serves to reinforce our sense of the mythic.

The themes of *Remembering Laughter,* like the technique, are simple, direct, and somewhat remote from ordinary life. At the focus of the novelette is the conflict between animal nature and human restraint that Freud explores in *Civilization and Its Discontents.* The poles of the conflict are embodied in the two sisters. Margaret is a creature of reason, conscience, restraint, convention — in a word, civilization. Her symbolic space is the guest parlor; she attempts, usually successfully, to impose discipline on what she finds uncivilized in her husband. But, if she controls herself and her world, order has a high price. She is unresponsive to what is vital in Alec, and late in the story we discover that she is incapable of bearing children. Her actions, grounded in morose puritan scruple, bespeak a neurotic aversion to the animal in human nature.

Elspeth, Margaret's polar opposite, is optimistic, unrestrained, impulsive, passionate; and she flies headlong into a world that is not nearly so innocent as she imagines it. Her qualities are more appealing than her sister's, but no less limited. If Margaret is altogether too precise about the distinction between nature and civilization, then Elspeth's error is the failure to recognize that such a distinction exists. Her mistake is harmless, even attractive in a naive sort of way, when she berates an amorous rooster: "You Mormon, you. You Brigham Young!" (36). But there is a hint of something more ominous in her suggestion that Alec should slaughter a brood sow that has devoured all but two of her litter. She fails to see that animal actions are unlike human actions in their consequences. Little wonder, then, that she is so helpless in the face of what is brutish and uncivilized in Alec. Elspeth generates new life, but hers is a creation destructive of human well-being, of laughter. It is a theme as old as Genesis, as contemporary as Freud: the human failure to reconcile the contradictory claims of animal nature and law is all too often the key to our undoing.

We began by remarking that *Remembering Laughter* exhibits several qualities characteristic of Stegner's later work. It remains to add that other elements in the novelette — elaborate structure, heightened prose, mytho-philosophical theme — are seldom found in his later long fiction. Why? We can move toward an answer by pointing to some of the problems in the book. The strong thematic contrast between the sisters, while successful in its mythical dimension, is too neatly dichotomous to earn the suspension of our disbelief. Malcolm is so thinly described that he has little more than symbolic import. And, if Stegner's grand theme tends to foster lifeless meanings rather than living characters, it also invites jargon. We hear too much about psychic repression and puritan aversion in *Remembering Laughter.* The tone of the writing is delicate, remote, and therefore difficult to sustain. At its best, it is pleasantly mellifluous over short stretches. At its worst — when Stegner loses control — it can be as obscure and spineless as this: "The shame was upon her, and with the ring of the pail in her ears she stood fixed in a sad catalepsis, wide-eyed staring, the gloom of the darkening barn a gelid medium supporting the shadowy thrust of stalls in a long row like the piers of ruined bridges jutting into a river of liquified dark" (90).

It may be that the weaknesses of *Remembering Laughter* are almost inevitable in brief novels in which the impulse toward the mythic is strong. We have discussed the book at some length, in part because it is a qualified artistic success, and in greater part because it allows us to observe our author experimenting with a type of fiction not altogether compatible with his talents. The experiment continued in Stegner's second novelette, but this time the results were disastrous. *The Potter's House,* published in 1938, is a sentimental rendering of the trials and tribulations of a deaf artisan and his family. The books' utter improbability, a key element in its failure, can be traced to the fact that the story has no apparent connection to the events or loci of Stegner's background. *Remembering Laughter* was made out of materials from closer to home, which helps to account for its success. *The Potter's House,* on the other hand, was remote from Stegner's experience; it strikes us as "made up."

Stegner seems to have recognized that he was quite literally out of his element in *The Potter's House.* If we look ahead to the very different novels that followed we can see that this failure taught its author several things. To write successful novels, he had to come up with interesting, plausible stories; and he must have recognized that the best stories he knew sprang from very personal memories. Finally, if he gave the matter conscious consideration, he realized that such stories did not invite elaborate technical effects. More storyteller than poet or maker of myths, more comfortable with narrative than with symbol, Stegner recoiled from what is decidedly artificial in his first novel and from what is painfully so in his second. Though not an important addition to American literature, *The Potter's House* is an important turning point in Stegner's career. The novels that follow it are longer, much more realistic narratives with deep roots in personal experience.

III   *New Directions*

During the weeks following Christmas vacation, 1938, Stegner interrupted work on *The Big Rock Candy Mountain* in order to compose his third novel, *On a Darkling Plain.* Published serially in 1939, and as a book in 1940, the story grew out of Stegner's reflections on his boyhood in Saskatchewan. What emerged was the story of a young, much decorated, but also seriously wounded veteran of World War I who lived in an isolated shack on the plains outside of East End. Disillusioned with war and with human inhumanity in general, he dropped out of society and sought solitude amid scattered homesteads on the bleak Saskatchewan prairie. Had it not been for the flu epidemic of 1918, he might have found what he was looking for. As events developed, however, the disease invaded his remote retreat, and his lungs. Someone brought him into East End, his condition grew worse, and he died.

It was a fine story, but it had no logical place in Stegner's main project, *The Big Rock Candy Mountain.* Still, it must have seemed especially resonant in 1938 when European conflicts threatened to engulf the entire world. Once again total war was imminent; once again the dark themes of conflict, of senseless aggression, and of man's inability to live in peace with his fellows forced themselves into the public consciousness. There can be little doubt that Stegner viewed his recollections of this romantic solitary in the light of current events. Nor can it be doubted that the fiction he made out of memory represents a response to those events. The theme is war; the problem is how an idealistic individual can accommodate himself to perpetual conflict. Edwin Vickers, the hero of *On a Darkling Plain,* a victim of gas and shrapnel in European trenches, withdraws from a hostile world to a lonely sod cabin on the Saskatchewan prairie. Vickers is a scarred veteran, but he is also a poet with a reputation for "running from realities."[2] Grim experience has persuaded him that warfare is the condition of all men in all societies. Angrily disillusioned, he succumbs to the skepticism of Matthew Arnold's "Dover Beach," the poem in which Stegner found the title for his novel:

> Ah, love, let us be true
> To one another! for the world, which seems
> To lie before us like a land of dreams,
> So various, so beautiful, so new,
> Hath really neither joy, nor love, nor light,
> Nor certitude, nor peace, nor help for pain;
> And we are here as on a darkling plain
> Swept with confused alarms of struggle and flight
> Where ignorant armies clash by night.

Arnold's poem in Vickers' hands amounts to a pacifist credo of noninvolvement. For Stegner, it appears, its corollary in the late 1930s was the anticapitalist, antiwar sentiment of Marxist intellectuals, the "beautiful thinkers" who so annoyed Bernard DeVoto.

Below the quotation from Arnold on Stegner's title page is a line from Archibald MacLeish's "Speech to those who say Comrade" which appeared in *Public Speech,* a slim volume published in 1936: "Men are brothers by life lived and are hurt for it." This line, the third in the poem, reads in partial context

> The brotherhood is not by the blood certainly:
> But neither are men brothers by speech — by saying so:
> Men are brothers by life lived and are hurt for it.

The verses are rather obviously addressed to Marxists and fellow travelers — to "those who say Comrade." The radicals, MacLeish suggests, are vendors of hollow words; they imagine that brotherhood results from merely "saying so." To the contrary, he replies, real brotherhood is the reward for shared labor, pain, and suffering. With Arnold, MacLeish portrays human life as a grim battlefield; but he insists that involvement in harsh realities, not withdrawal into romantic nostalgia and beautiful words, is the key to genuine fellowship: old soldiers are the best friends. The poem is characteristic of MacLeish in the late 1930s: it is an urgent call to arms, a passionate public confession of belief in democracy as muscular unselfishness, a thing of good deeds, not words. He concludes:

> Brotherhood! No word said can make you brothers!
> Brotherhood only the brave earn and by danger or
> Harm or by bearing hurt and by no other.
>
> Brotherhood here in the strange world is the rich and
> Rarest giving of life and the most valued:
> Not to be had for a word or a week's wishing.[3]

Bernard DeVoto would have agreed with Arnold and MacLeish that life is a constant struggle; but DeVoto would have taken MacLeish's side in insisting that valor, not retreat, is the proper response.[4] Stegner's Edwin Vickers arrives at the same conclusion, but not until the closing pages of *On a Darkling Plain*. At the outset he is a romantic recluse. Outfitted with supplies and a volume of poetry, he puts the hateful society of East End behind him. His mind is adrift on a raft of misconceptions: society is evil; nature is good; knowledge of self is most accessible when one is isolated from others; he is self-sufficient; sexual urges are unimportant; solitude is desirable.

The romantic in Edwin Vickers is gradually but ineluctably washed away. Erosion commences when he finds that he cannot establish himself on the prairie without help. Abel Sundstrom, a reticent, generous neighbor, brings strong arms and experience to the construction of a sod cabin. Ina, Sundstrom's daughter, invades Vickers' privacy with questions and his repose with naive but frank enthusiasm for his company. Communication is established when she persuades him to respond to her daily smoke signals. Uninvited, she brings him a cake and stays to dinner. To her suggestion that it is not quite human to live alone and unproductive on the plains, he replies feebly: "I don't think most people are human" (45). Gradually, however, her candor and simplicity begin to penetrate his skeptical veneer. Reluctantly he acknowledges that he enjoys her company, that smoke signals are something to look forward to, and that sexual urges are far from unimportant.

Another neighbor who instructs Vickers in the potential dangers of solitude is Kenny Wilde, a lecherous misfit, who lives in squalor a few miles south. Luring Vickers to his hovel, he proudly displays his collection of dirty pictures. Vickers recoils in disgust, but not without registering the impact of Wilde's perverted example. Retreat into nature, it appears, is not necessarily a source of purification. Nor, Vickers discovers, is solitude under an enormous sky the beginning of self-knowledge. At times he hates "the vast earth. It was too big and too impersonal; it dwarfed him, made his very consciousness seem sick, as if he were the one spot of corrupt tissue in a mighty health" (110). Unhappy with people, but equally unhappy with his isolation, Vickers falls far short of the stoic resolution that he had anticipated. "That was a dream of Arnold's, that self-dependence, that sanity. It was a dream, not possible of realization, another statement of man's aspiring credulity. On the breast of that vast impersonality he saw himself, a tiny, gesticulating ape with the god in him surging toward magnanimity and peace, and the weakness of the flesh like a chain on the ankle" (121).

Bracing himself against the collapse of his illusions, Vickers gets down to the practical business of preparing for winter. He rejects Sundstrom's advice to move into town; he can bear the cold, and the news of an approaching flu epidemic strikes him as just another good reason to avoid people. But Ina's distress signal and her hysterical disclosure that Kenny Wilde has brought the plague to the Sundstrom farm, mark the beginning of the end of his exile. Concern for Ina, loyalty to her father, and the simple instinct to provide assistance take Vickers back to East End and to a society more literally sick than the one he abandoned.

The appalling spectacle of a remote village caught in an epidemic sends Vickers spinning through a cycle of epiphanies. The Sundstroms' predicament forces the bitter admission that "You couldn't stay out of it. You couldn't stay out of anything" (169). Even the despicable Wilde has a claim on his compassion. The example of selfless Dr. O'Malley and a few sleepless days and nights of caring for the sick give Vickers "a good feeling of comradeship, the sense of working hard with other people in a common cause" (188). But the shock of Ina's terrible death completely turns him around. His incipient feelings of brotherhood are smothered under an avalanche of suicidal despair. Once more his world is reduced to the warfare "of starving men feeding on each other, too vicious to be even pitiable" (206).

Having buried Ina, disconsolate, he wanders into the woods and happens upon a most improbable tableau: a trapper is drowning a mink in the rapids of a stream. Vickers protests, but the man persists in his cruelty. Walking away, Vickers suddenly discovers a parable in what he has just witnessed:

Up through him then, with a surge that lifted him to his toes in the bitter snow, came the fighting determination to live — what for, to what end, for whom, he didn't know. His mind had made that decision automatically in · that vision of drowning by the rapid; now it came stronger. He would fight whatever it was that put men in a life painful to bear, and dared them to bear it. He would bear it, by God, if only to give the owner of the strangling hands pneumonia, keep him out at his little game so long that he died of it himself. (210)

Vickers' blind determination to endure in a malignant universe is only the penultimate stage in his moral progress. At the novel's close, suffering from a furious attack of flu, he decides that fear is the crucial constant in human life. For the craven mob — those who shrink from brotherly action for fear of consequences — he has nothing but contempt. He reserves his esteem for people who overcome fear, who defy the whimsies of fate and inscrutable death. Such people, Vickers assures himself, possess true valor, for they bring decency and compassion to the service of humanity. Such, in brief, are the major steps in his journey from Arnold to

MacLeish. Faint but resolute, Vickers rises from his cot to help bury the dead.

Summary has the effect of highlighting the weaknesses of *On a Darkling Plain* and of obscuring its genuine strengths. To be sure, the defects of the novel are very real and perfectly obvious. The mink episode is the most glaring lapse. How is it, we wonder, that this heartless trapper musters enough energy and will to carry on during a flu epidemic? Wholly improbable, a kind of morality play, the incident is much too contrived to bear the weight that Stegner places upon it. With the other defects in the novel, this melodramatic diversion seems to be the result of hasty workmanship. Too often in *On a Darkling Plain* Stegner settles for ingenious and rather lame literary short cuts. The mink is one instance, and the heavy reliance on "Dover Beach" in the portrayal of his protagonist's state of mind is another. Vickers' long letter to his old friend Bob, in which he summarizes most of the principal themes of the novel, is a third.

The letter points to another major problem in *On a Darkling Plain* — overstatement of theme. In this novel, as in several others, Stegner makes the mistake of allowing his characters to reiterate and make explicit what is implicit, but perfectly obvious, in the action. The delicate treatment of Ina's innocently frank eroticism is flawed by an episode in which she rechristens one of her dolls Vickie (for Vickers) and locks it in an embrace with another doll, Celia. Abrupt shifts in point of view are equally heavy-handed, and they arise from a similar failure to leave well enough alone. When Dr. O'Malley reflects, "There was something about Vickers that calmed you down" (183), it is Wallace Stegner we hear, not the village physician.

If *On a Darkling Plain* is marred by the products of hasty composition, and by what we may call thematic overkill, it is also Stegner's remarkably successful first attempt to deal with an extended, realistic narrative. There is a confidence in this third novel that is lacking in the first two, a confidence that stems from Stegner's close personal acquaintance with his material and that takes its most striking expression in the novel's freedom from artifice. Stegner is at home in this landscape; he knows its moods and colors and wildlife. His characters are the denizens of boyhood memory; they are fully conceived and credible. For the first time, dialogue is plentiful; salty, abrupt, colloquial, it rings true. The prose keeps to the ground, drawing its color from the region, its people, and their common speech: "All the way up the dugway road he kept his head twisted to look out over the curves of the valley, a steep-sided, flat-bottomed ditch like the trail of a dragged hoe" (9).

That they are overstated from time to time does nothing to diminish the fact that the themes of this novel — centering on Vickers' conversion from misanthropy to a sense of brotherhood — emerge rather effortlessly from the unadorned narrative. Curious, optimistic, fresh and open, Ina is perfectly plausible as a provincial farm girl; and, at the same time, she is an ideal foil to Vickers' bitter cynicism. Her pleasing forwardness, her naive questions, and her healthy sexuality generate the tensions that force Vickers to reenter society. Her father's tight-lipped dignity, and his unquestioning good will, contrast effectively with Vickers' sullen, suspicious reticence. Kenny Wilde is first and foremost a contemptible prairie rat. Thematically, however, he functions as a paradox. On the one hand, he symbolizes the pervasive spiritual disease that prompts Vickers to withdraw from human society. On the other, Wilde's contamination of the Sundstroms is the occasion for Vickers' return to East End and is, therefore, a key factor in the tempering of his misanthropy. Finally, Stegner makes good use of the contrast between the catastrophes of war and plague: the first, of human design, drives Vickers into exile; the second, a natural disaster, drives him back to the world of men. This brief catalog is hardly exhaustive, but it should provide a rough index to the richness that Stegner discovered in this brief episode from his youth.

On a Darkling Plain does not belong on the shelf of Stegner's best books. Among his first four brief novels, however, it stands out as the one that most clearly anticipates his earliest major success, *The Big Rock Candy Mountain*. The principal elements of *On a Darkling Plain* — setting, characters, language, some of the events, and realistic treatment of a story drawn from recent, personal history — anticipate the longer, more important novel. The book is early proof of a point that Stegner would later insist upon — that you write best about what you know best. His fourth offering, *Fire and Ice,* lends negative confirmation to the same point.

Wallace Stegner describes his fourth novel as a look at the Madison Young Communist's League. Material and inspiration for *Fire and Ice* resulted from attendance at a few of the organization's meetings while he was still teaching at the University of Wisconsin. The book was dashed off in a matter of weeks and published in 1941, not long after the Stegners arrived in Cambridge.

The title of *Fire and Ice* points to the qualities of desire and hate that merge in its hero, Paul Condon. A product of Depression poverty, a poor student who holds down four jobs in order to pay his way through school, and a member of the Young Communist's League, Condon's personality is a thin fabric of contradictions. He hates capitalism, the middle class, and the well-heeled students from that class who make their way across campus in tweeds and furs. His fury focuses temporarily on a graceful skater who dips and spins in short skirt and tights across a university rink. "Good, Paul thought. No false moves there. Graceful, sure. Then he caught up with himself. A dressed-up capitalist doll showing off her legs."[5] Condon, who has not had a date in two and a half years, fails to recognize the portion of downright lust that fuses with his hatred. *Fire and Ice,* desire and hate: Paul Condon craves the affluence and social prerogatives of the bourgeoisie at the same time that he despises them.

Condon's relationship to his Marxist peers is equally ambiguous. In touch with the rudimentary formulas of the League — prolabor, anticapitalism, antiimperialist war — he is astute enough to admit that the Nazis may be something of a threat. But Condon is too prone to violence, too much an irascible individualist, to be of any use to the movement. He looks for fights, finds them, and thereby earns a stern lecture from Willem Trapp, an old union laborer. "This-here Party," Trapp warns, "is bigger than any man in it. It's bigger than any personal ambitions you got, or any personal love, or any personal hate. . . . I think maybe you got the idea the Party exists so you can satisfy your personal dislike of capitalism. You don't like to do things the way the Party votes them. You hate taking orders" (129–30). Trapp's admonishment fails to impress Condon. If the Party dislikes the way he does things, the Party can go to blazes.

As the conclusion to a series of improbable coincidences, Condon finds himself alone in his room with Miriam Halley, the graceful skater. She wants an interview for the school paper on how the other half lives. The encounter ends abruptly when the young radical, suffering from the effects of too much alcohol and too many years without a date, nearly succeeds in raping his visitor. He wakes up in jail. Contrite, horribly hung over, he is suddenly possessed with astonishing self-knowledge. He sees that poverty frustrated his ambition to be a big shot; that frustration issued in hostility and paranoia; and that Miriam "was the symbol of everything you hated and wanted. So you tried to rape her, because rape is a kind of murder and a kind of love" (193). Finally, when preparing to catch a ride out of town, he explains to a friend that the Party may have been responsible for his close scrape with the law. Marxism, he argues, is a credo of ready-made answers and opportunistic methods. His biggest error, he concludes, "was not to know myself better. And no amount of economics would have taught me that" (213). Convinced that there are more important things than money, he walks away.

There can be no doubt that Stegner found the title for *Fire and Ice* in a poem of the same name by his friend, Robert Frost. Published nearly twenty years before the novel, Frost's "Fire and Ice" is a potently epigrammatic glance at the forces of desire and hate. The poet, who shared DeVoto's regard for the sturdy yeoman farmer and who took a dim view of the New Deal, would have agreed with Paul Condon's conclusion about Marxism and money. Our point here is simple enough: *Fire and Ice* is at one important level an ideological novel. And, we imagine, its generally anti-Marxist drift would have been acceptable to men like Frost, DeVoto, or, for that matter, Archibald MacLeish. But ideology, as this novel well illustrates, is not easily transformed into art. Strong ideas, in any but the most skillful hands, tend to flatten character and to distort plot. Ironically, *Fire and Ice* shares in most of the deficiencies that Professor Rideout has noticed in its political counterpart, the proletarian novel of the same period: pointless violence, melodrama, falsification of character, recurrence of stereotypes, "wish-fulfillment" endings, and a tendency "to tamper with the logic of the novel's own structure of relationships."[6] In brief, *Fire and Ice* reads more like an argument than a story.

As art, then, the novel is about as close to failure as Wallace Stegner has come. Moreover, because it tampers with the internal logic of its plot, *Fire and Ice* strikes us as a confused, and, therefore, as a weak argument. As Paul Condon hitchhikes out of the novel, it is quite clear that we are meant to approve his decision to abandon radical politics in order to seek self-knowledge. It seems equally clear that our agreement with his view of the Young Communist's League — "something like mysticism" (212), with dogmatic answers and unscrupulous tactics — is taken for granted. But if we agree with Condon, what are we to make of Willem Trapp, perhaps the most sympathetic character in the novel? Reasonable, patient, hardly a mystic, Trapp is portrayed as altogether dignified and humane in his objectives. Given Trapp's example, Condon's characterization of the movement, and his decision to ignore it, are at best premature, at worst, extremely poor judgment.

Furthermore, Condon's assertion that "there are worse things than being poor" (212) would be plausible on almost any lips but his own. He has forgotten what we cannot help remembering: the grinding poverty of his youth; his father, who was injured in a strike and took three years to die; his poor mother, who worked her knuckles raw for twenty-three cents an hour; the rich, arrogant college brats who add humiliation to the already intolerable hardships suffered by poor students; fatuous Junior Leaguers like Miriam Halley; the fact that a wealthy nation tolerates gross social and economic inequities; and that those in turn produce humorless, violent neurotics like himself.

If we accept Condon's conclusions, then we must also turn a blind eye to the very real political problems that *Fire and Ice* sets forth. True, he will do well in tending to his mental health; but to suggest — as he does, and as the novel does — that his problems are merely psychological, is to utterly deny what his experience has made patently obvious. Since his pathetically limited social and economic opportunities have made him what he is, the novel violates its own internal logic by closing with the strong suggestion that its protagonist's problems are all due to marginal mental health. We come away with the feeling that Condon's quest for self-knowledge is a step in the right direction, but that his search will be frustrated until he recognizes that his personal unhappiness is ultimately rooted in the unfair distribution of social and economic opportunities. In short, we are left with the impression that Condon could make a truly significant step toward self-knowledge by having another chat with Willem Trapp.

At the beginning of our discussion of *On a Darkling Plain,* we drew some lines between the themes of that novel and the political persuasions of Archibald MacLeish and Bernard DeVoto. Substituting Frost, we have drawn similar but clearer lines to the themes of *Fire and Ice*. In spite of Stegner's allusions and themes, however, these novels are, in a rather peculiar way, apolitical. We can begin to unravel this apparent paradox if we draw out some of the implications of Stegner's failure to send Paul Condon back to Willem Trapp. Like Vickers, Condon is alienated from society because of his inability to accept things as they are. In Stegner's view, human beings and human societies are alike in their "cussedness." Add the belief that men are slow to change, and you have the rudiments of his philosophy of life. A question follows. How do such attitudes dispose their possessor to the world of politics? Our answer is hypothetical and somewhat complex. That political scheme which promises to preserve things as they are, or, preferably, which encourages reform at a pace consistent with human inertia, is applauded. On the other hand, political schemes which promise radical change are condemned on two counts: first, man and society being what they are, radical changes are unlikely to occur; second, such schemes make people unhappy by inflating their expectations. It should be added that political activities in such a scheme are relatively unimportant: they reflect what is characteristic of society, but they can do little to change it. If we assume that this roughly approximates his political philosophy, then it is not surprising that Stegner did not send Paul Condon back to Willem Trapp. Trapp is a good man, but there is little he can do to alter things as they are. Radical change being an impossibility, psychological adjustment to the status quo is at a high premium. Condon's only practical recourse is to attempt to bring his expectations into realistic alignment with things as they are. That, at least, seems to be the significance of his rejection of the Young Communist's League and his decision to concentrate on changing himself, not the world.

On a Darkling Plain and *Fire and Ice* are apolitical, then, to the extent that they envision a world of static political and social arrangements in which the drive for substantial change always succumbs to the necessity for individual adjustment to the status quo. Society, inequitable and diseased as it is, remains the same; Edwin Vickers and Paul Condon change. If Stegner's attitudes seem conservative, then his variety of conservatism springs from a powerful intuition about the human condition. Stegner's world is as uncompromising and bleak as the Saskatchewan prairie. It has its moments of magnanimity and peace; but, as Vickers learns, its principal themes are conflict, suffering, catastrophe, and death. The corollary in *Fire and Ice* to Vickers' hard lesson is Condon's discovery that *a priori* logic and "beautiful" ideas can lead to gross self-deception. Some will agree with Stegner's decision not to send his hero back to Willem Trapp; some will not. The question is ultimately of secondary importance, for the novel's very real deficiencies are aesthetic, not philosophical. Were Condon more distinct as a character, questions of ideological purport would not dominate the critical foreground. It remains true, however, that readers will vary in the degree to which they can accept the far-reaching implications of Stegner's dark view of the human condition.

IV   *Triumph:* The Big Rock Candy Mountain

If, as we have suggested, Wallace Stegner's political values are not the function of unaided logic but the offspring of a compelling intuition about the condition of man, then his fifth novel is the record of the background to that intuition. *The Big Rock Candy Mountain* is the nakedly autobiographical account of the childhood and youth behind the man. The novel is set in the landscape that repelled Vickers; forever flat under the dome of an eternal sky, impersonal, extreme, hostile to human wishes, it is the Stegner country. North Dakota, Saskatchewan, the Great Salt Lake Valley, in such places, particularly during the years of Stegner's youth, the conditions of life were harsh and uncompromising. The principal characters in the novel — Bo Mason (Stegner's father), Elsa Mason (his mother), Chet Mason (his older brother), and Bruce Mason (himself) — respond to the land and to the experience it witnesses and partially determines in different ways. Of the four, however, three have at least one important response in common: prematurely, brutally, they die. Chet is the first to perish. Defeated, barely a man, he succumbs to pneumonia. Bo is last. Solitary, hopes and illusions shattered, he puts a bullet through his ruined mind. Some years earlier, Elsa is mutilated and finally annihilated by cancer. In Bruce's eyes, the disease is a hideous emblem of what is common enough but totally unacceptable in life.

A body completely replaced itself in seven years, but that was done to pattern, according to a plan. This was something else, an insane crowding of formless hostility, a barbarian invasion, blotting out the order and the form and the identity, transforming it into a shapeless thing that was not his mother at all, but an unidentified colony of cells, functionless and organless and hopeless. For one blasted moment he stared at her in panic, almost expecting her to bulge and puff and swell, lose her features, change into a grotesque horror before his eyes.[7]

Her disease symbolizes all that threatens order, coherence, personal identity, a sense of place and security in space and time. More concretely, more immediately, more painfully, it destroys forever what is loved beyond expressing. Brutal, final, without consolation, death moves with authority in Stegner's view of the human condition.

The Big Rock Candy Mountain is much too long and far too complex for summary here. Moreover, summary would be repetitious; most of the essentials of the story appear in the first chapter of this volume. The novel telescopes the events of about forty years — beginning with Elsa's flight from home and ending with Bo's suicide — into something closer to thirty. The principal effect of this truncation is to leave Bruce Mason younger and less certain about the shape of the future than Stegner was at the time of his father's death. One thing, however, is perfectly clear to Bruce: he must "try to justify the labor and the harshness and the mistakes of his parents' lives" (515). The publication of The Big Rock Candy Mountain in 1943 represented a large installment on that debt to the past.

Young Bo Mason — handsome, energetic, violent, self-deceived, a wanderer, emotionally incapable of accepting responsibility — introduces size and motion into a novel that we value for its possession of precisely those qualities. Bo makes The Big Rock Candy Mountain go. Though enormous, his energy is finite. His gradual decline is of the highest thematic significance; the dream of adventure and easy money is an illusion fed by his unrealistic optimism and restless gusto. As energy fades, the dream fades, to be replaced by bitterness and despair. Pursuing a phantom territory where "you stood on your own two feet and to hell with the rest of the world" (93), he sacrifices his family, ignores the law, severs his connection with society, and squanders his great potential. A variation on a theme by William Gilpin, his life exemplifies the waste of human and natural resources that hollow myths and unchecked individualism have meant to the West.

It is a familiar argument that Satan is Milton's real but un-acknowledged hero in *Paradise Lost*. A version of the same argument applies to *The Big Rock Candy Mountain*. Like Satan, Bo is awesome, fiercely proud, resourceful — he makes things happen. He has a "sultry and almost dangerous charm, a feeling of power you got from him as you got heat from a stove" (102). By far the most successful part of the novel — the first three-quarters — is narrated almost entirely from the point of view of Bo or Elsa. Writing with great confidence, Stegner recreates the excitement and frustration of rural life in the first decades of this century. His theme — the struggle between radically opposed domestic and social values — is unobtrusive, nascent in the conflict between Elsa and Bo. Because they lend depth to the portraits of the protagon-ists, because they intensify our sense of conflict and inevitable disaster, and because they do not come heavily freighted with obvious thematic significance, the numerous shifts in point of view are smooth and effective.

Here, for the first time, and for hundreds of pages, Stegner achieves "the middle ground." Dramatic, a plausible fiction rooted in history, his narrative articulates important Western continuities. Bo's restless energy and individualism are the psychological ves-tiges of a vanished frontier. Elsa's reflection that he should have been born a hundred years earlier could not be more apt. As it is, his personality is a tragic anachronism. Qualities such as Bo's were an asset in the opening of the West, but their useful role in its his-tory was brief. Once opened, the frontier cried out for different things: for law and cooperation and planned settlement. That such social virtues did not prevail, that the frontier mentality outlived its usefulness, and that Powell lost out to Gilpin are familiar Western themes. They come alive in Bo Mason.

For more than half of the novel Bo shares the foreground with Elsa. No less a Western type than her husband, she is a latter-day representative of the feminine, civilizing impulse that was persist-ent, if relatively unsuccessful, beyond the hundredth meridian. Gentle, domestic, long-suffering, a buffer between her sons and their irritable father, she opposes the rootless impermanence and antisocial individualism of her husband. The word closest to Elsa's heart is "home": "Home, as she imagined it and remembered it, had always meant those things, children, permanence, the recur-rence of monotonous and warmly-felt days, and animals to care for'' (87). Bo is an insurmountable obstacle to the fruition of her desires because he cannot appreciate what Elsa knows, that ''a home had to be lived in every day, every month, every year for a long time, till it was worn like an old shoe and fitted the comfortable curvatures of your life'' (227).

Far more sympathetic than Bo, Elsa is somewhat less successful as a character. Once she is married, we see little of her positive qualities — her vitality, good humor, and readiness to be pleased. Incapable of containing Bo, her role is the negative one of tedious, dogged resistance. A much more telling defect is the glaze of sentimentality that deepens in Elsa's characterization as the novel progresses. For obvious reasons, Stegner found it difficult to achieve the same detachment with Elsa that he did with Bo. Indeed, he locates the precise source of the problem when he has Bruce reflect that his memories of Elsa ''were probably colored by a sentimental pity that had little relation to his mother's real feelings'' (350). Understandably, the sentimental tone becomes more marked as Elsa's death draws nearer and as Bruce's point of view becomes dominant.

In an astute and positive review, Howard Mumford Jones describes *The Big Rock Candy Mountain* as ''a vast, living, untidy book.'' He points to ''the living force of the narrative'' and the reader's strong impression ''that a whole world has arisen out of nowhere around him.'' Jones quite properly emphasizes the spaciousness of the novel, its plentitude of apt detail, and its full evocation of regional life. In the midst of much that is praiseworthy, however, he locates one major fault. The reflective manner that Bruce adopts in the final third of the novel jars, he argues, ''with the geniality and strength of the rest of the narrative.''[8] We would add that the problem goes deeper than style.

No doubt as the result of his close identification with Bruce's point of view, Stegner allows him to speculate at great length on the significance of his family history. The result is unfortunate, for well-paced, thematically coherent narrative gives way to imperfectly disguised commentary about that narrative. Bruce keeps a journal in which he poses crucial questions — ''What is my father? What is my mother? What is my brother? What am I?'' (403) — that are followed by eloquent, detailed answers. Later, at his father's funeral, he again provides the reader with a summary analysis of the meaning of Bo's life. At another juncture he generalizes from his own past to the history of the country: "Those were the things that not only his family, but thousands of Americans had missed. The whole nation had been footloose too long, Heaven had been just over the next range for too many generations" (424). All of this would be more acceptable if Bruce stumbled occasionally, thus introducing an element of irony into the reader's perspective on his reflections. But Bruce rarely falters. At one point he chides himself: "Who are you to philosophize about the problems of a nation?" (426). Such moments are rare. All too often, in artificial devices like the journal, or in long soliloquies, Bruce hammers home what the narrative has already made perfectly clear.

The final chapters of *The Big Rock Candy Mountain* slip from "the middle ground" because they record a very personal authorial response to persons and events in the Mason family history. Such reflective endings may have their place in literature, but in this case the effect is to upset the delicate balance of action and theme that Stegner maintains in the first three-quarters of the novel. As we have seen, the problem is not unique to *The Big Rock Candy Mountain;* but the problem is less critical because this novel is otherwise masterfully executed and because we value Bruce's meditations for the very considerable light they throw on Stegner's conception of things as they are. Brutal death, as we have noted, is central; but, despite its cruelty, death defies home. Returning to his father's funeral in Salt Lake City, Bruce realizes that "there was no doubt where his home was, because part of him was already buried in those two graves and in two days another part — admit it — would be buried in the third."(504-5).

Although death annihilates his family, it fails to break the continuum of generations that links Bruce to the past. A man, he decides, "runs through his ancestors" (403). Bruce adopts this position at his peril, for his family record, and the larger record of Western experience which Bo and Elsa exemplify, is a chronicle of waste, violence,and blighted hopes. Boldly, he accepts the facts and dilates upon them. The personal present, the living, conscious ego, is merely the sharpest edge of history, formed and impelled by the past, wedging its way into the future. Change is gradual, a slow evolution of elements beyond the individual's control. The past, harsh and painful as it is, must be studied, for in its continuities we discover the stuff and shaping energy from which we are made.

Experience makes a conservative of Bruce. Things as they are defy Bo's grandiose illusions just as relentlessly as they frustrate Elsa's desire for home and peace and culture. There is little reason to anticipate radical changes in that pattern. Affirming what he can in his parents' lives, acknowledging the rest, Bruce turns a tentative but hopeful eye to the future: "Perhaps it took several generations to make a man, perhaps it took several combinations and re-creations of his mother's gentleness and resilience, his father's enormous energy and appetite for the new, a subtle blending of masculine and feminine, selfish and selfless, stubborn and yielding, before a proper man could be fashioned" (515).

The Big Rock Candy Mountain was received, and doubtless it will be reread and remembered (the novel was reissued in 1973) in a variety of different contexts. In the most general terms, it is an extended, almost epic commentary on the great American dream, one first fully articulated by Thomas Jefferson, of a massive national migration to the wild, fertile, nearly endless territory to the West. For more than a century that dream was a constant of the American consciousness. Born out of pride, acquisitiveness, a sense of national purpose and destiny, an agrarian ideal, a love of wide spaces, open and free, and a longing for purification and redemption, the dream lured millions like Bo and Elsa across the continent. Even for Americans like Herman Melville, who resisted the pull, the frontier was the symbolic stage where a hopeful, exhilarating, definitive national drama would unfold itself. Though Stegner's chapter in the frontier story is a rather late one, it combines the energy, high aspiration, violence, frustration, failure, and renewed though qualified hopefulness that were characteristic almost from the beginning.

More narrowly, *The Big Rock Candy Mountain* has retained a reputation as a classic of American regionalism. Early reviewers were especially responsive on this score. "Wallace Stegner's latest book," observed Joseph Warren Beach, "shows great advance in power and grasp over the shorter novels for which he is chiefly known, and is a much more satisfying example of regional fiction."[9] Another reviewer located the source of the novel's success in Stegner's close familiarity with regional life and landscape: "He knows the West not as a traveling salesman but as a boy who was born there, who knows the look and smell of the Mormon country, who knows how to use his hands and where the big fish are to be caught.... He has an unquenchable appetite for the little villages of Dakota, the deep woods of Washington, the raw spots of Saskatchewan — where our rovers still go."[10]

Such praise was well deserved. For precise and faithful evocation of place, *The Big Rock Candy Mountain* has few equals. Through Elsa's eyes we see the dusty desolation of a North Dakota town just after the turn of the century:

The main street was a river of fine powder between the raised plank sidewalks. On both sides a row of hitching posts stood in vanishing perspective down to the end of the street, which trailed off weakly into open country. As she walked, looking for her uncle's store, Elsa saw with sick certitude that Hardanger was ugly. Frame buildings, false fronts, gaping vacant lots piled with old barrels, boxes, blowing newspapers, ashes. Dust-choked streets and sidewalks that were treacherous to walk on because sometimes the ends of the boards were loose. A general store whose windows were crammed with overalls, pitchforks, gloves, monkey wrenches, spools of barbed wire, guns, boxes of ammunition, ladies' hats. A butcher shop and bakery under the same roof, the windows of both opaque with fly specks. On the first corner a two-story frame hotel, its windows giving her a momentary glimpse of leather chairs and a disconsolate potted palm. A drug store across the street, its sides plastered with advertisements for medicines. Next to that a vacant lot, then a pensioned railroad car set end-to to the street and wearing on its front the legend "Furs bought for cash." Another vacant lot, a store labeled "Gents and Ladies Haberdashery," a billiard hall and bowling alley, and then her uncle's store: "Karl Norgaard, Plain and Fancy Groceries." (24–25)

With Bruce we experience the hopefulness that accompanied the rainfall on the Saskatchewan prairie in the good summer of 1915:

Things greened beautifully that June. Rains came up out of the southeast, piling up solidly, moving toward them as slowly and surely as the sun moved, and it was fun to watch them come, the three of them standing in the doorway. When they saw the land east of them darken under the rain Bo would say, "Well, doesn't look as if it's going to miss us," and they would jump to shut windows and bring things in from yard or clothesline. Then they could stand quietly in the door and watch the good rain come, the front of it like a wall and the wind ahead of it stirring up dust, until it reached them and drenched the bare packed earth of the yard, and the ground smoked under its feet, and darkened, and ran with little streams,and they heard the swish of the rain on roof and ground and in the air. (187)

Finally, *The Big Rock Candy Mountain* has an important place in the ranks of American fictional autobiography, for it is Wallace Stegner's *Huckleberry Finn*. Naturally, it is difficult to make a clear separation between what is national, regional, or simply personal in a novel as fully integrated as this one. Indeed, we would value it less were such distinctions easily made. At the least, however, we can say that Wallace Stegner's early life was a complex sequence of powerful and sometimes painful experiences which he subsequently transformed into a novel that provides us with illuminating perspectives on American history and the American consciousness. We would merely add that the pace, range, and thematic coherence of *The Big Rock Candy Mountain* are the offspring of experience carefully scrutinized and deeply felt. The novel's energy and permanent relevance seem to have issued from a perceived conjunction of the personal with the national past. Stegner must have recognized, as Bruce Mason certainly does, that his own experience could be viewed as an important expression of larger American continuities. In this light, then, and without diminishing the fact that it is a superb transformation of raw memories, *The Big Rock Candy Mountain* arrives at "the middle ground" because Stegner had been there all of his life.

V   Second Growth: *a Diversion*

Wallace Stegner tells us that he wrote *Second Growth* during the school year of 1945–1946. The book was published twelve months later. On the one hand, *Second Growth* appeared roughly midway between the publication of what Stegner himself calls his first two "full-length" works of fiction: *The Big Rock Candy Mountain* (1943) and *The Preacher and the Slave* (1950), which we discuss in the final pages of this chapter. On the other hand, *Second Growth* was sandwiched between two projects in sociology: *One Nation* (1945) and the abortive comparative analysis of village democracy which Stegner began and abandoned in 1953. Moreover, *Second Growth* was written during Stegner's most prolific period as an author of short stories; indeed, a brief section of the novel appeared separately in the *Virginia Quarterly Review* in 1943.[11]

To be brief, *Second Growth* shares both the virtues and the defects of its most proximate literary siblings. Parts of it — those parts which most closely resemble Stegner's past successes in dramatizing personal experience — are characteristically good. Other parts, which reflect their creator's contemporaneous journalistic enterprises, appear in rather unhappy contrast to the robust narrative of *The Big Rock Candy Mountain*. As a whole, the book cannot be accounted a success. Instead, we must see it as a temporary lapse into the kind of thematic overstatement that mars *Fire and Ice*. It is unfortunate that *Second Growth* did not remain what it evidently started out to be — a loosely connected series of short stories recounting the business of growing up in a rural backwater.

The central character in *Second Growth* is not a person but a place: the village of Westwick, New Hampshire, during the period just after World War II. Once a model of New England self-sufficiency, the dilution of the ethos of old Westwick can be traced to the day that Stephen Dow, a distinguished historian, settled on the village as the site for his summer retreat. Other university types soon follow. This rather specialized group of tourists — known to the Westwickers as the "summer people" — are determined to preserve the venerable simplicity of their adopted community. Over the years, however, their presence brings change. As *Second Growth* opens, Westwick is discovering that it has gradually become a summer resort — a rather select and snobbishly exclusive one, to be sure, but a summer resort nonetheless. Sensitive to outside encroachment, the local residents' association vetoes movie houses, and the local inn turns away Jewish lodgers. But certain developments cannot be reversed. The time-honored village vocations of agriculture, husbandry, and craftsmanship are no longer viable.

Eighty-year-old John Mills, the quintessential small-town artisan — honest, kindly, reticent, deeply committed to the high quality of his work — is the only surviving representative of his breed. James Mount, the talented musician who should have been John Mills' successor, is old at fifty, a disreputable drunkard exhausted by the hard work and paltry rewards of a collapsing economy. A haven for affluent outsiders, Westwick holds out diminishing opportunities to its permanent residents. *Second Growth* suggests some answers to the problems of this village in transition by tracing the careers of a few of its most promising young people. Andy Mount, Helen Barlow, Abe and Ruth Kaplan — all combine respect for Westwick with a keen awareness of its limitations.

Helen Barlow, the town's only recent college graduate, is the daughter of one of Westwick's most prominent families. Bored with the village, she is nevertheless too timid, too morbidly self-absorbed, to move away. Like her father, a self-proclaimed and malingering paralytic, Helen's response to the frustrating limitations of provincial life is withdrawal. But compromise and retreat prove impossible, even in sleepy Westwick. When Flo Barnes, a beautiful and aggressive lesbian, arrives in town for the summer, Helen is fascinated with "the woman's tidal strength and confidence."[12] Drawn to Flo, yet fearful of ostracism by a disapproving community, Helen's unstable truce with Westwick collapses under the weight of irreconcilable impulses. She resolves the dilemma by withdrawing more completely than ever, into suicide.

Abe and Ruth Kaplan also find frustration in Westwick, but for the opposite reason. If the village is a kind of jail for Helen Barlow, it is an impregnable fortress for the Kaplans. Jews, orphans, and political refugees, they have never experienced a permanent home. They are eager to enter the common life of the village, but local religious intolerance and racial prejudice stand in their way. Only the sophisticated "summer people," who recognize the intelligence and integrity beneath the Kaplans' unfamiliar exterior, treat them with the respect and affection they deserve. When Helen Barlow commits suicide by drowning, Abe and Ruth make a heroic but futile attempt to rescue her. Such manifest good will softens the prejudice of their neighbors, but the Kaplans remain isolated on the margin of the community. They discuss the obvious question but never resolve it to the reader's satisfaction: are the pleasures of Westwick as great as the sacrifices they entail?

This question puzzles Andy Mount, the most successfully realized character in the novel. A younger son of the disreputable Mount family and a town ward since the age of ten, Andy is well acquainted with the social injustices and limited opportunities of life in Westwick. But he is also familiar with the positive aspects of the rural experience: independence, a stable system of values, the gratifications of labor on the land. Finally, Andy is impressed with the example of Helen Barlow, who is painfully alienated from Westwick society as the result of her college education: "She was neither village folks nor summer folks; she had been successfully educated away from her own life but not into the other" (123).

When Peter Dow, the headmaster of Dryden Academy, offers him a prep school scholarship, Andy hesitates to accept. Dow is encouraging and to the point: "you just can't develop far enough in a society this narrow and this static" (62). But not until John Mills suffers a stroke and Helen Barlow commits suicide is Andy jarred into a decision. At the novel's conclusion he is on a train to Dryden Academy, exhilarated by the prospects ahead, but acutely conscious of the good he is leaving behind: "He went willingly, even eagerly, but he went with the spectral taste of ripe blackberries on his lips and with his eyes already homesick for the autumn woods and the mown meadows and the tarnished silver farms, for the limited responsibilities and the worn-out obligations and the narrow security that it would be fatal to accept" (240).

In surveying the early novels we have learned that Stegner is most confident when he deals with a familiar place and when he keeps his eye on what is indigenous to that place. In *Second Growth,* there are well-conceived, credible characters like Andy Mount and John Mills who spring to life in Stegner's imagination and in his prose, just as surely as the landscapes of their native region. On the other hand, Flo Barnes and the Kaplans are as completely beyond Stegner's artistic range as they are outsiders to the Westwick area. Psychologically shallow, implausible in their actions and speech, they function principally as pawns in the novel's too obvious thematic play. Such characteristic strengths and weaknesses are apparent in the novel's closing sentence, excerpted above. Stegner's "autumn woods," "mown meadows," and "tarnished silver farms" hint clearly enough at what Andy values in Westwick, and at what finally drives him away. But delicate subtlety vanishes with the intrusion of "limited responsibilities," "worn-out obliga-tions," and "narrow security." Two-dimensional stereotypes such as Flo Barnes and the Kaplans are aesthetically defective in the same way, but at a different level. At its best *Second Growth* develops themes that are regional in the deepest sense — literally true for one particular spot of ground, they are widely applicable, on a more symbolic plane. Stegner seriously weakened the novel, however, by settling too often for flat characters and prose in which the suggestiveness of art gives way to bald, rather commonplace sociology.

VI   The Preacher and the Slave

Before turning to Wallace Stegner's partially fictional treatment of him as a character in *The Preacher and the Slave,* let us consider a few facts and questions relating to Joe Hill.[13] Born in Sweden in 1879, Joel Hägglund was a quiet, musical child. Shortly after the death of his mother, he emigrated to the United States in 1902. He came expecting to find gold in the streets. Accounts vary, but it seems clear that his first few years in this country were disillusioning ones. At first young Hägglund worked at odd jobs in New York; sometime later he was fired and put on a blacklist for trying to organize laborers in Chicago; he changed his name to Joe Hill (he was also referred to as Joseph Hillstrom) and moved West to Washington, California, Hawaii, possibly to Mexico; he appears to have joined the Industrial Workers of the World (Wobblies) in San Pedro, California, in 1910. During the next few years he became well known for such union songs as "The Preacher and the Slave," "Casey Jones — the Union Scab," "Workers of the World, Awaken!" and many others which appeared in the Wobblies' "Little Red Song Book."

But the troubadour of a singing union did not begin to achieve international fame until he was arrested on January 13, 1914, in Salt Lake City. Found wounded in a boardinghouse, Joe Hill was charged with the murder of a grocer and his son. His alleged accomplice, Otto Applequist, was never found. The litigations over the next two years were extremely complicated. Hill claimed that he was shot in a quarrel over a woman. Arguing that it was the state's task to establish his guilt, he refused to identify her, and she failed to come forward. He was executed on November 19, 1915.

The case of Joe Hill was an international *cause célèbre.* Appeals came from such notables as President Wilson, Helen Keller, Samuel Gompers, and W. A. F. Ekengren, the Swedish Minister to the United States. The Wobblies, who rallied to his defense, were convinced that their songster was the innocent victim of Mormon capitalists hostile to their organization's agitation. The union lost the legal battle, but they elevated their hero to martyrdom after his death. "Joe Hill's Last Will," written the day before his execution, is a masterpiece of artless simplicity and a key element in his legend.

> My will is easy to decide,
> For there is nothing to divide.
> My kin don't need to fuss and moan —
> "Moss does not cling to a rolling stone."

My body? Ah, if I could choose,
I would to ashes it reduce,
And let the merry breezes blow
My dust to where some flowers grow.

Perhaps some fading flower then
Would come to life and bloom again.
This is my last and final will.
Good luck to all of you.

Joe Hill

But legends simplify; they persist only because certain questions are forgotten or overlooked. "The question of Joe Hill's guilt or innocence," concludes Gibbs M. Smith, "is no more certain today than it was in 1915. After reviewing all available records, however, there is considerable reason to believe that Hill was denied justice in the courts of Utah, and that there was still reasonable doubt as to his guilt after the district court and the supreme court had consigned him to the firing squad.''[14] He may have been a double murderer, but most observers agree that he was convicted on inadequate circumstantial evidence. A clear motive was never established; the "why" remains unclear; the problem is reduced to what one makes of the man himself. Taciturn, solitary, was Joe Hill the noble soul that the Wobblies have made him? Or was he the killer that the courts of Utah sent to the firing squad? Double murderer or martyr, that is the issue.

In retrospect, it is not difficult to explain Wallace Stegner's interest in this controversial figure. Joe Hill was a Scandinavian, an immigrant from Sweden; he was a songster with a cause; he made his mark in the West; he was executed in Salt Lake City. In the first of two essays about Joe Hill which appeared before the publication of *The Preacher and the Slave* (1950), Stegner describes the famous Wobbly in terms that apply equally well to Bo Mason: he was "a certain type of Western badman, with a pleasant manner, an immaculate exterior, and a lot of cool nerve."[15] To be sure, there are important differences between the two men — for example, Joe was a loner who avoided women, liquor, and tobacco — but the similarities are much more striking. They were both dreamers; both had a knack for lyrics; both (according to Stegner) were prone to violence; both operated outside of the law; both struggled against things as they are; both died frustrated in the city of the Saints.

In the second and longer of his essays, published in the *New Republic* in 1948, Stegner addresses himself both to the Industrial Workers of the World and to their martyr. Marxist and militant, advocates of class warfare and the abolition of the wage system, the Wobblies were bent on revolution. In the light of Stegner's previous pronouncements on radical movements, his hostility comes as no surprise. Never sympathetic to labor agitation — an attitude he shared with Bernard DeVoto — he condemns the Wobblies as "a direct-action movement, believing in sabotage and violence."[16] The context established, he turns to Joe Hill: "What is actually known of him, what can be found out? Who was he, what was he, and how accurate is his legend?"[17] The questions were rhetorical, for Stegner had done plenty of homework.

Stegner's analysis is grounded on interviews and extensive correspondence with old Wobblies, several of whom knew Joe Hill, and on careful study of the records of the trial.[18] Conclusions follow in rapid order: "As for Joe Hill, I think he was probably guilty of the crime the state of Utah executed him for, though I think the state of Utah hardly proved his guilt beyond a reasonable doubt." He argues that the state's failure to establish a motive is not "a sure sign that no motive existed." Rejecting Joe Hill's story that he was protecting a woman, he goes on to relate that "every old-timer I have found who knew Joe Hill admits that he was a stick-up man." Violent crook that he was, however, the Wobbly troubadour was easy "to blow up to martyrdom because he had the poet's knack of self-dramatization." Especially in his "Last Will," and in the many telegrams that he composed during the final days of his life, Joe Hill laid the foundation for his own fame and martyrdom. "These are the words and acts of a great natural showman, the infallible raw materials of legend, and they are in themselves almost sufficient explanation of how an obscure dock worker and sailor, a nameless stiff, a crude poet and mushy writer of sentimental songs could also be the François Villon of American labor."

In the midst of this damning assessment of Joe Hill, we come upon a most startling assertion: "It doesn't really matter what he was."[19] In view of Stegner's questions about the man, and more especially in view of his answers, the statement appears to be a contradiction. Somewhat in spite of himself, however, Stegner the essayist elects to emphasize the important fact of a persistent legend rather than the complicated personality of the man behind it. This much notwithstanding, the reader cannot fail to recognize that what Joe Hill did and why are the issues that caught the novelist's imagination. He confronts those issues, the "what" and "why" of the Wobbly martyr, in *The Preacher and the Slave.*

The obstacles to success in Stegner's seventh novel were enormous. That he was sensitive to the difficulty of the task is clear enough in the foreword to *The Preacher and the Slave,* for Stegner insists that his novel "is not history, though it deals here and there with historical episodes and sometimes incorporates historical documents; and it is not biography, though it deals with a life. It is fiction, with fiction's prerogatives and none of history's limiting obligations. I hope and believe it is after a kind of truth, but a different kind from that which historians follow." Glancing at the "ambiguous personality" of his protagonist, Stegner concludes that "Joe Hill as he appears here — let me repeat it — is an act of the imagination."[20]

There can be no doubt that Stegner was wise to disclaim any pretense to historical or biographical accuracy. The facts about Joe Hill are too scarce, and the accounts of his activities too contradictory, to permit a definitive analysis of his personality. It follows — as Stegner appears to acknowledge — that any sharp portrait of the martyr (or murderer) will amount to a fictional extrapolation based on a careful, even partisan, sifting of the evidence. Stegner's essays about Joe Hill reveal that he came to the novel with clear ideas and settled opinions about his subject. As some of his earlier works indicate, however, strong prepossessions sometimes lead Stegner into thematic overemphasis, simplification, and jarring authorial intrusions. His principal problem in the novel, therefore, was to apply imagination to a strong and controversial interpretation of Joe Hill without appearing to intrude upon the narrative and without allowing the weight of his prepossessions to flatten character into caricature. In short, to succeed in *The Preacher and the Slave,* Stegner had to overcome his own greatest artistic weaknesses.

In almost all respects he was successful. Joe Hill, as Stegner represents him, is the violent, at times sentimental, self-dramatizing personality we meet in the essays. According to Stegner, he carries a gun; he is a thief; and his thoughts and actions, most of them the creations of Stegner's interpretive imagination, are permeated with violence. "I want to die a martyr" (323), he tells the Pardon Board, and another crucial element in Stegner's interpretation of the man takes fictional confirmation. But, if imagination constructs an irascible felon and a self-generated martyr, it also envisions a talented, intelligent, sometimes gentle man whose human potential is blocked by vague fears and by a crippling sense of personal inadequacy. Joe Hill, we feel, is basically a good man whose background and circumstances combine to bring out what is weakest in his nature.

Moreover, Stegner's potent descriptions of unemployed workmen struggling for survival in a San Pedro slum, or of grossly underpaid migrant workers living in squalor outside of Sacramento, go far to account for Joe's hatred of "the system." True, the Wobblies emerge as an organization that "really liked a fight better than it liked planning, negotiations, politicking" (ix). True again, Joe's capacity for self-deception and his inclination to violence are given much greater emphasis than his more positive qualities. But even those who disagree with Stegner's interpretation of the man and the movement will concede that his fictional reconstruction is a plausible, extremely well written, compelling "act of the imagination." Since the truth of the case is beyond recovery, no fictional treatment of the subject can do more.

The key to the success of *The Preacher and the Slave* resides in Stegner's skillful handling of four distinct points of view. The novel is framed in two brief sections narrated by an eloquent, occasionally ironic Wobbly. Looking back on the period of Joe Hill's execution, the narrator, a nostalgic believer, reflects, "We were rich in martyrs then" (1). Distilled and softened by time, vague as a cloud, his Joe Hill is myth pure and simple. The omniscient narrator is heard second. His principal function is to set scenes, to introduce characters, and to relate the larger human movements (strikes, riots, public reactions) surrounding Joe's life. This voice is at once absolutely necessary to the novel and potentially its greatest weakness: necessary because it provides "objective" descriptions of Stegner's acts of imagination; potentially a weakness because Stegner might have violated the illusion of neutrality essential to this voice by using it as a mouthpiece for his own interpretation of Joe Hill. Generally, the omniscient narrator is detached; he describes from the "outside." Occasionally he intrudes. Joe Hill, he tells us, is "a man who never led with his tongue; a counterpuncher strictly. . . . A singleton, a loner, a man with a hot temper and no really close friends. But a rebel from his skin inwards, with an absolute faith in the One Big Union and nerve enough for five. . . . What called him, speaking a language he understood perfectly, was trouble. Where trouble brewed, he appeared" (107). Such moments, when Stegner speaks too directly and when the reader feels the pressure of judgments not adequately accounted for by his experience of the narrative, are relatively few.

If the omniscient narrator provides fictional resolution to the "what" questions of a martyr's life, then those portions of the novel which present Joe Hill's point of view address themselves to the "why." From beginning to end, Stegner's treatment of his protagonist's thoughts, motives, and fantasies is impressive because it records a consistent, organic, and therefore plausible development. At the outset Joe is a quiet, lonely man whose anger has not yet found an outlet or a specific object. Later, thanks to his songs, he is welcomed into the union, which provides both. But his involvement in union agitation is disillusioning; he discovers that "every strike and brawl and revolution and mass meeting ended the same way, in a choice between being a willing sacrifice for no real purpose, and running like a scared animal when the law moved in" (152).

More angry and violent than ever, but also more alone and penniless, Joe arrives in Salt Lake City "without a clear destination or a clear purpose except the restless and never-satisfied purpose of striking a blow, keeping a promise, exacting a partial vengeance" (193). Blind lust for revenge and the need for money are the motives which make him vulnerable to Otto Applequist's suggestion that they rob a local merchant. In thus resolving the "why" question, the novel provides fictional justification for the clear implication that Joe Hill was a double murderer. The concluding chapters trace the sequence of rationalizations and seemingly willful self-deceptions which persuade the killer that he is actually cut out for martyrdom.

Finally, there is Gustave Lund, a benevolent Lutheran minister who runs the Scandinavian Seamen's Mission in San Pedro.[21] Lund's role in the novel is manifold. A pacifist, a skeptic resigned to things as they are but ever hopeful of gradual change, at the thematic level Lund represents the Christian alternative to Joe's militancy. At another level, and to the degree that his observations duplicate those to be found in the novelist's essays about Joe Hill, he seems to function as Stegner's alter ego. "The Wobbly movement," he muses, "what made it attractive to men like Joe Hill-strom, was that it was no program at all. It was as reflexive as a poke in the nose, and about as constructive" (187). Later, he raises strong objections to "the story Joe told about the woman: anyone who knew Joe Hillstrom would instantly doubt it" (255). Such speculations would strike us as authorial intrusions were it not for the fact that they are perfectly natural in a man of Lund's background and character. Moreover, although Lund raises intelligent questions about Joe, he is much less ready with answers than Stegner the essayist. Lund is completely undecided; indeed, he is the only nonpartisan observer in the novel. Patiently, with all the objectivity he can muster, Lund searches for the truth about Joe Hill. His questions go unanswered. At the execution we find him still puzzled over his enigmatic friend. "As the white-haired doctor bent forward with his stethoscope to his ears to examine the heart of Joe Hill, workman and singer and rebel, hero now in a hundred IWW halls, either a martyr to law's blindness or a double murderer, Lund examined that heart in another way, and could not find the answer he searched for" (401).

At the conclusion of *The Preacher and the Slave* Lund moralizes about the Wobblies who roar like "an angered animal" outside the prison walls. "For them, at least, there were no complications, no querying of the demands of vengeance, and justice, and love" (402). In the absence of clear answers to the "what" and "why" of Joe Hill, the preacher refuses to take a final position. The reader, it appears, is being invited to join Lund in his rejection of partisan-ship and in his resignation to ambiguity. In short, the preacher's moral seems to bear the stamp of Stegner's approval. Paradoxi-cally, however, while Lund's ultimate uncertainty is justified, the reader's is not. As we have indicated, the narrative of *The Preacher and the Slave* bears the crystal clear implication that Joe Hill assisted Otto Applequist in the robbery and homicides for which he was tried, convicted, and executed. Lund has no access to this information; therefore his uncertainty is warranted and just. For the reader, however, there is neither uncertainty nor ambiguity. Joe Hill, according to the interpretation presented in Wallace Stegner's novel, is guilty as charged.

Can we account for this curious inconsistency? Is there any way to square Lund's seemingly definitive moral observations with the contradictory evidence provided by the preceding narrative?

Probably not. Apparently Stegner nodded. On the other hand, it may be that the lapse is not without its special significance. Perhaps it brings us back to a point that we made at the beginning of this chapter: that in our analysis of human motivation we must settle for uncertainties. Or, perhaps the inconsistency is a reminder that the assignment of guilt, even when it is established beyond a reasonable legal doubt, is a pragmatic judgment made by men, of other men. It does nothing to explain or alter the mysterious human capacity for evil. Perhaps, too, it is Wallace Stegner's inadvertent admission that he was not as sure about Joe Hill as he thought he was.

CHAPTER 5

A Shooting Star,
All the Little Live Things, *and*
Angle of Repose

I *Change and Continuity*

THE bibliography of Stegner's publications at the back of this
volume is a heterogeneous document, but at least one pattern
immediately strikes the eye. After the publication of *The Preacher
and the Slave* in 1950, the Stegner record is bare of novels for well
over a decade. The reasons for this lacuna are not difficult to un-
cover. An unusual hybrid of history and literature, *The Preacher
and the Slave* met with a mixed critical reception. Predictably, the
radical press flayed it for daring to debunk one of labor's holy martyrs. The few more moderate publications that noticed the novel
generally praised it; but, for the most part, Joe Hill's fictionalized
biography was resolutely ignored by the critics. Silence, we are
told, is more painful than criticism. Not surprisingly, sales were
poor. As a writer used to commercial and critical acclaim, Stegner
found the silence and slim sales extremely discouraging. His dis-
couragement ran deeper for the fact that he considered *The
Preacher and the Slave* his second attempt at a full-length novel,
the only major work on the shelf beside *The Big Rock Candy
Mountain*. As the result, Stegner devoted the next decade to other
varieties of literary endeavor. He nurtured the Stanford Writing
Program, turned out some first-rate journalism, published his
Japanese literary lectures, the Powell biography, and a dozen short
stories. But between 1950 and 1961 he avoided the critical gauntlet
that he was bound to run if he brought another novel before the
reading public.

The 1961 publication of *A Shooting Star* marks Stegner's return to the major novel; happily, it was also a return to commercial triumph and to a qualified but tolerable critical success. As a Literary Guild selection, *A Shooting Star* quickly reached sales of more than one hundred and fifty thousand volumes — figures which doubtless did much to salve the bruises suffered with the poor reception of *The Preacher and the Slave.* It was followed by *All the Little Live Things,* which appeared in 1967, and the Pulitzer prize winning *Angle of Repose* four years later. No doubt additional novels will follow. For the purposes of critical argument, however, we are forced to ignore the fact that the Stegner canon is still growing. In this final chapter we will proceed as though *A Shooting Star* and its two successors were Stegner's final works of fiction.

Chronologically, these three works are separated from Stegner's previous novels by a chasm of eleven years; in the areas of subject, setting, and narrative voice, they represent an equally significant departure. Apparently pleased with the technical success of "Field Guide to the Western Birds," Stegner continued to make good use of first person narration. All three of his latest novels deal to a greater or lesser extent with life in California, Stegner's ultimate home — with its remarkable landscape, its indigenous character types, and unique forms of social organization. On the other hand, all of the volumes refer to values and life-styles characteristic of other parts of this country, occasionally to evoke an ideal, more often to establish a measure for cultural comparison. In the same vein, each of the novels is firmly rooted in the contemporary world; yet in two of the books vivid recreations of the American past function as background to, and as a yardstick for, present-day life. This balancing of past and present is not a new feature in Stegner's writing. Rather, it is the clearest possible evidence that he has persisted in his idealization of "the middle ground." Because these novels represent regional and technical variations on familiar themes, they are as important a series of stops along the trail to "the middle ground" as *The Big Rock Candy Mountain* and *The Preacher and the Slave.* Indeed, the final member of this trio, *Angle of Repose,* marks its creator's arrival at the very center of that elusive territory.

II   A Shooting Star

A Shooting Star has roots in both nineteenth-century New

England and contemporary California. It is when these roots are most intricately intertwined that the book is at its best. Stegner found the material for his eighth novel in a most uncharacteristic margin of California — on the Gardner Hammond estate, an exquisite reproduction of a New England mansion, situated in Montecito, just outside of Santa Barbara. The Stegners were intermittent guests in Montecito from the fall of 1944 to the spring of 1945, the peripatetic academic year which preceded their permanent settlement at Stanford. From this privileged vantage, Stegner had ample opportunity to observe the behavior of California's "idle" rich; and, thanks to Mrs. Hammond, he also had access to more unusual and less contemporary data — the history of this curiously anachronistic estate, its present inhabitants, and their forebears.

The rather complex action of *A Shooting Star* brings both aspects of Stegner's Montecito experience to fictionalized fruition. Personal acquaintance with the dissatisfied socialites of Santa Barbara (and, later, with their unhappy equivalents in Palo Alto) results in the portraits of Sabrina Castro, her society physician husband, and other denizens of their glamorous but empty world. On the other hand, Stegner's more or less historical acquaintance with Mrs. Hammond and her departed forebears gives rise to Sabrina's mother, Deborah Hutchens, and to other twisted branches of her family tree. As we have indicated, the interaction between the several Hutchens generations, living and dead, is the key to what is successful in the novel.

Sabrina Castro, the central character in *A Shooting Star,* is an attractive, wealthy young California aristocrat. To any unbiased observer, she appears to enjoy the best of several different worlds. The only female descendant of an old and at least financially distinguished New England family, the Wolcotts, she is the present possessor of more dollars than she knows what to do with and heiress to many millions more. She is also the wife of one of the last of the "Californios," the original, native-born Californians of Spanish-speaking descent. Finally, Sabrina is a beauty, and a beauty of an especially memorable kind. Long, lean, fine-boned, and graced with extraordinarily mobile and expressive features, she is instinctively feminine, irresistible, a charmer. But despite, or perhaps because of, her advantages, Sabrina is deeply, even desperately unhappy. Sterile, and therefore deprived of the loving

labors of child rearing, she sees herself as no more than an orna-
ment to her husband Burke's fancy Pasadena medical practice. In
Sabrina's eyes, Burke is not a healer. Rather, somewhat unjustly,
she regards him as chief handholder and pill-dispenser to a flock of
wealthy female hypochondriacs. Sabrina subjects her New England
ancestors to similarly harsh and reductive scrutiny. From her point
of view they appear to have been the stunted progeny of American
puritanism; among other things, they were acquisitive, self-
righteous, uncharitable, and self-absorbed.

Despite an expensive education and a fast-paced, sophisticated
youth, Sabrina has achieved neither self-knowledge nor a clear
sense of what she wants from life. Her story is dominated by two
images: the mirror and the mask — images which are inversely
related. The mirror implies an obsession with self, the mask, real
uncertainty as to what that self may be. When she is (all too frequently) alone, Sabrina spends an inordinate amount of time looking at her own image in some reflective surface: mirror, car
window, picture window, silver teapot. Even Burke's proposal, as
she remembers it, is framed within the borders of an old pier glass.
On the other hand, every time we find Sabrina in company, we
catch her playing a part: virgin or vamp, sin-struck adultress or
existential heroine, anybody but the complex mixture of qualities
that she really is. In short, fifteen years past adolescence, this dis-
contented beauty is finally beginning to experience what psychologist Erik Erikson has called the "identity crisis."

The first half of *A Shooting Star* is the record of Sabrina's moral
disintegration. In Stegner's suspenseful opening chapter, we gradually discover that Sabrina has jeopardized her enviable personal
advantages by indulging in a sordid and unsatisfying affair. Even
after she recognizes the limitations of her lover, she resists reconciliation with Burke and continues to confront him with new and
increasingly painful humiliations. It all culminates in a classically
"lost" weekend which she spends slumming among the bars and
barflies of Carson City, Nevada. Having hit bottom, Sabrina
recognizes her severely limited options: she can go up or out. The
rest of the novel chronicles her slow return to psychological
stability and personal integrity.

After the collapse of her marriage, Sabrina has no recourse but
to take refuge on her mother's luxurious old estate, her childhood
home. Living there, she naturally encounters some of the figures

influential in her early years: mother, brother, best friend, favorite family retainer. Each of these individuals has, in his own way, confronted the problem of personal identity. Each illustrates a different response to the questions that Sabrina has been asking herself: what is personal identity? and what does one do with one's life? As soon as Sabrina stops looking at herself long enough to observe those around her, she discovers that some of her childhood fellows have created a satisfying life for themselves, and that others have not. If the difference between the two groups is clear, so is the bearing of the situation on Sabrina's own future. She can be happy and useful only if she is willing to abjure both the sybaritic self-indulgence and unrealistic expectations that Stegner calls "ecstacy,"[1] and settle instead for the limited gratifications of "a halfway decent life" (422).

The wasted lives of her departed Wolcott relations provide Sabrina with another important set of moral *exempla*. The Wolcotts have traditionally resolved the identity crisis in the simplest and least satisfactory manner: by ignoring it. In some respects, it was unfortunate for his descendants that great-grandfather Cornelius was a natural born money-maker. Thanks to his prodigious financial exploits, by the end of the nineteenth century the Wolcotts had amassed a considerable fortune. However, none of them had learned how to deal with the opportunities and responsibilities of affluence. The family failed to develop a tradition of community service; neither philanthropists nor artists nor promoters of culture, they found no socially or personally productive outlet for their money. In the lives of Cornelius' children and only grandchild, Deborah Hutchens, wealth operated as a shield against the larger world and, paradoxically, as an obstacle to personal growth.

Nevertheless, at the beginning of the novel Sabrina's mother is proudly aware of her background: she is a Wolcott of Beacon Street. Family history is Mrs. Hutchens' consuming passion. Her Hillsborough home is a perfect replica of the old Wolcott retreat at Nahant; her conversation is a self-conscious pastiche of reminiscences and hoary anecdotes. Sabrina feels that her psychological development was hopelessly perverted by growing up in this atmosphere of oppressive reverence for the past; her Wolcott aunts and uncles siphoned off the uncritical and unqualified affection that she herself deserved as Deborah Hutchens' only daughter. Absorbed by memories of rejection, Sabrina has never examined her mother's life carefully enough to resolve the obvious contradiction: if the old lady loved and identified with her Wolcott relatives, why did she leave them?

Newly sensitized by her personal difficulties, and living at home again, this time as an adult, Sabrina begins to unravel the mystery. Her mother's "ancestor worship" is not the single-minded enterprise that it had seemed. Deborah Hutchens loved her husband Howard, in spite of, or perhaps because of, the "vulgar" vitality that offended the rest of the family. When he committed some infraction of their marriage bond, she hewed to the Wolcott line and left him, but with deep and deeply buried feelings of resentment. The separation accomplished, she retreated to the West Coast, ostensibly to avoid scandal, actually to avoid further confrontation with dubious family mores. Having allied herself irrevocably with their values, she was also able to see those values for what they were: small-minded, self-righteous, and pharisaical. Finally enlightened, Deborah was also helpless to change. Despite her fabulous fortune, the opening of *A Shooting Star* finds her a lonely and defeated old woman. Her daughter sees her as a psychological adversary; to her son, she is the chief obstacle to the profitable operation of the Wolcott estate. In the absence of her children's forbearance, Deborah takes consolation in the prepaid affection of her secretary-companion, Helen Kretchmer.

It would be unfair to describe Oliver Hutchens, Deborah's son, as a malicious man; he is simply morally incomplete. Sabrina rightly calls him a "somatotonic" (139) — a purely physical human type. Despite a total lack of planning, Oliver's life has been as orderly as Sabrina's has been chaotic. He succeeds at each stage in his development because his objectives are clear and simple and unchanging: to compete and win, to accumulate material goods and enjoy them, to keep himself moving for the sheer pleasure of watching his muscles work. His current economic campaign against his own mother is a case in point. In his peculiar way, Oliver loves Deborah Hutchens and wants nothing but the best for her; unfortunately, he has his own terribly limited definition of "the best." To be brief, Oliver is prepared to have his mother declared incompetent in order to gain control of the estate and make her, as he puts it, "a hell of a lot richer" (336). Fortunately for Mrs. Hutchens, an unexpected ally enters her life and opposes Oliver. Leonard MacDonald, the husband of Sabrina's best friend, suggests an entirely novel plan for the disposition of the Hutchens property: why not set aside some of the acreage as a public park?

The example of the MacDonalds represents an instructive contrast to traditional Hutchens values. Strong, competent, tough-minded, Leonard has worked his way up from the slums to an instructorship in English at the local high school. With three small children to support, he is forced to live in Greenwood Acres, the quintessential mass-produced American tract; but, like Joe Allston, he makes the best of "middle-class civilization." Leonard's dedication to cooperative community betterment exemplifies the only hopeful alternative to suburban individualism. If any Americans ever learn to sacrifice present profit for the benefit of posterity, it will undoubtedly be the inhabitants of Greenwood Acres. In Leonard's words, "we're already living in the over-crowded future and we know how it feels" (102).

The MacDonalds have planned their own future with unusual foresight and wisdom. Leonard enjoys the rewards of excellence in his professional career; nevertheless, he does not expect individual achievement to satisfy all of his inner needs. Two other types of activity — activities notably missing in Sabrina's life — are equally important. First, there is participation in the ancient, repetitive, mysteriously fulfilling cycle of procreation and child rearing. Second, there is participation in the slow but steady course of community improvement. As Leonard tells Sabrina, "It's funny how many different kinds of things you can make a halfway decent life out of if you believe in them and work at them. Likewise it's funny how no combination really turns out to be exactly the Kingdom of Heaven" (422). This measured compromise between optimism and pessimism, a familiar element in Stegner's work, is at the core of the MacDonald philosophy.

In the final chapters of *A Shooting Star,* with Leonard as her guide, Sabrina begins the transition from hollow "ecstacy" to "a halfway decent life." First, she acknowledges that she is as much to blame as Burke for the disintegration of their marriage. Recognizing the extent of her own conjugal errors, she considers returning to Pasadena and resuming the role of the society physician's wife. But this rather improbable scheme dissolves when she discovers that she is pregnant with an illegitimate child. Dismayed, but unwilling to admit defeat, Sabrina has at least learned that cooperation and compromise with others are essential to personal happiness.

Accordingly, as the second stage in her program for self-improvement, she focuses her attention on her mother and on her own unborn offspring.

Helen Kretchmer, Sabrina realizes, can never provide the filial affection and support that her mother so clearly requires. Nor can Helen protect Mrs. Hutchens from Oliver's insensitive designs. Sabrina resolves to supplant Helen, to become the daughter that her mother desires, and to thwart her brother whenever possible. At the same time, she will try to raise her fatherless child according to the somewhat smug MacDonald formula for family happiness: "love but not too much love, and not the wrong kind" (422). It is a challenging objective, but not an unrealistic one, especially if pursued on a steady, day-to-day basis. Together, grandmother, mother, and child may be able to break the twin chains of guilt and resentment that have shackled the Wolcotts and replace them with ties of understanding and love. Then, reaching outward from a secure base in familial affection, they will readily develop the sense of civic responsibility that their inherited fortune demands. In Stegner's view — a view explicit in the MacDonald philosophy, and implicit in Sabrina's conversion — family support and cooperation are the essential first steps toward participation in the larger human community.

A Shooting Star closes with Mrs. Hutchens' moving memory of childhood disappointment — what we may call the parable of the pink balloon. Walking one day in the Boboli Gardens, six-year-old Deborah accidentally loses her grip on the most beautiful balloon in the city of Florence. Her mother sternly refuses to replace it. "If there is one day in my whole life I would not . . . want to live over ! If there is . . . one day that sums up everything!" (430) she exclaims in a voice resonant with seven decades of imperfect resignation. A trivial loss by all accounts, but with that balloon went the ecstacy in Deborah Hutchens' life. Sabrina listens, understands, recognizes what she shares with her mother and, through that sense of common loss, finds consolation and resolve. Thus the novel's final affirmation arises from the discovery of historical continuities: Sabrina gains a future by uncovering a usable past.

Most readers will agree that the contemporary characters in *A Shooting Star* — most notably Leonard and Oliver — come a little too close to allegory for comfort. They strike us as "thesis" characters — as embodied ideas that walk into Sabrina's experience at appropriate intervals. The novel, as a result, seems too direct and insistent in making its point. A rather contrived plot is also partly to blame. As Stegner put it in an interview with us, "there's a soap opera problem in *A Shooting Star*." Finally, the novel is marred by awkward inconsistencies in narrative point of view. At various junctures each of the contemporary characters assumes the mantle of omniscience just long enough to summarize the moral and thematic significance of one of his fellows. Leonard explains Sabrina, Sabrina explains Oliver, and so on.

It is also worth noting that this sort of thematic overstatement never occurs when Stegner is dealing with the ancestors of his characters. Our information about the Wolcotts is always second-hand; it is filtered through Deborah Hutchens' misguided idealiza-tion of the past, her daughter's neurotic contempt for it, or Leonard MacDonald's more moderate appraisal of things past. Glimpsed through several imperfect lenses, the background to the action possesses the essential complexity and ambiguity which the foreground lacks. At the end, the reader is left with the final responsibility; he must reach his own conclusions about the Wolcotts.

III   All the Little Live Things

Characteristically, Wallace Stegner's ninth novel existed first as a series of short stories; "Field Guide to the Western Birds" (1956) and "Indoor-Outdoor Living" (1959) provided *All the Little Live Things* with both a setting and a cast of principal characters. The place is familiar: a carefully protected, affluent bedroom com-munity on the exurban fringe of San Francisco that is modeled, quite obviously, on Los Altos Hills, California, Stegner's adopted home. More important, the narrator is Joe Allston, the engagingly irascible presiding genius of the Casement cocktail party. Neverthe-less, *All the Little Live Things* differs from its two fictional ante-cedents in tone and scope. In this more ambitious work, the dark side of Allston's sensibility — which Stegner has compared to the feints and jabs of a boxer defending a glass jaw — is clearly revealed. On one level, *All the Little Live Things* is an exploration of the so-called "hippy revolution" of the 1960s and the sub-sequent widening of the "generation gap." But this episode in the running war between the generations is arbitrated by a radiant young mother who is dying of cancer. On another, equally accessible level, *All the Little Live Things* is its creator's most straightforward, comprehensive meditation on the bleakness of the human condition since *The Big Rock Candy Mountain.*

Through the medium of Joe Allston, Wallace Stegner poses and attempts to resolve the ultimate human issues: life versus death, good versus evil, nature versus civilization, the mingled pleasure and pain of participation versus the dubious security of retreat. At the time of its publication, one reviewer complained that *All the Little Live Things* was overly dichotomous — "too schematic."[2] Though we have had occasion to make this criticism of previous Stegner novels, in the present case, we feel, it is unwarranted. The narrator, Joe Allston, retired literary agent and self-appointed custodian of middle-class values, is a compulsive categorizer of men and morals. His philosophical categories, it is true, fall into rather simplistic patterns of opposites; but, despite his shortcomings as a thinker, he is fully credible as a psychological type. In Joe Allston — dichotomies included — Stegner found the perfect vehicle for his special talents as storyteller, nature writer, and surveyor of the human scene.

All the Little Live Things begins with another of those suggestive, suspenseful, immediately engrossing prologues that have been Stegner's trademark since *Remembering Laughter.* In "How Do I Know What I Think Till I See What I Say?" the reader is presented with disconnected bits of information that he only gradually fits into a larger framework. Joe and Ruth Allston, a recently retired couple in their early sixties, have fled the rat's nest of Manhattan's literary underworld and reenacted the romantic myth of the Garden West by settling among the live oaks and fertile hills of Northern California. Joe is a skillful, dedicated, even passionate gardener, but, like many another Eastern expatriate, he has come to the Golden State in search of more than flowers, fresh fruit, and sunshine. In fact, he is seeking peace of mind.

The coddled son of an overworked Danish servant girl, Joe realized the American promise of social and economic success, but too late to lighten his immigrant mother's burden. His dealings with his only son were equally incomplete and unsatisfying. Curtis Allston, a professional nonconformist, antagonized and disappointed his father by flitting from one fashionable cause to another until a surfing accident (or was it suicide?) brought an abrupt end to thirty-seven years of strident discontent. Joe suffers

from a vague sense of guilt for the wasted lives of both his mother
and his son, but he fails to see how he could have treated either of
them differently. After several months of sleepless nights, and an
abortive trip abroad to reexamine his Danish "roots," he abandons
the attempt to understand his past and resolves to immerse himself
in California's perpetual present. As the primary action of the
novel begins, Joe and Ruth have settled into a busy but orderly
regimen designed to occupy the leisure hours of their old age. They
read and write, take long walks, and maintain a friendly but strictly
"cocktail party" relationship with a few neighbors. Mainly they
cultivate their garden.

Before long, however, the Allstons discover that they share their
little corner of Eden with a goodly number of unwelcome inter-
lopers. Even California's rich soil and mild climate cannot be considered unmixed blessings, for, as Joe points out, "Evil likes Paradise every bit as much as Good does."[3] If Allston plants a peach
tree, it immediately gets leaf curl; if he sets out a frame of tomato
plants, they attract gophers; and, when he tries to trap a gopher in
its underground passageway, he spears a friendly king snake
instead, a beautiful creature, and the natural bane of his garden's
pests. To Allston's instinctively allegorical imagination, colored as
it is by a deep sense of personal failure, the king snake's murder is
pregnant with meaning — "a riddling revelation of the inadvertent
harm we all do" (201). The moral he extracts from his garden is not
unlike the one that Edwin Vickers draws from the World War I
battle at Ypres. Life, Joe believes, is a Darwinian nightmare which
pits man against man, and man against beast, in a fierce but futile
struggle for survival. Personal security can be obtained only at the
expense of creatures less capable or less fortunate than oneself.
Although the constraints of civilization provide some relief and
must be preserved at all costs, it must be admitted that they are a
pitifully feeble bulwark against the brutality of things as they are.
The only solid defense is withdrawal, the kind of retirement to
which the Allstons have resorted. Bemused by such reflections, Joe
is forgetful of his chief complaint against his wayward son: Curtis
was a coward who never accepted his responsibility to confront
things as they are — "to be a man" (177). Not until two very different but equally disturbing human visitors invade the quiet of his
garden does Joe become aware of the inconsistencies in his
philosophy.

The first intruder is Jim Peck, a disaffected young student from the local university. Peck materializes on the Allston acres one sunny autumn afternoon complete with heavy beard, raucous motorcycle, and the standard intellectual baggage of the "hippy" revolutionary. He is disgusted with the sterility of contemporary education and wants to exchange crowded dormitories and establishment classrooms for a campsite on the Allston's unused river bottom, an ideal spot for "sanyasi" meditation. Prompted by his guilty memories of Curtis, and urged by Ruth, Joe gives reluctant consent. He sees Peck as a modern Comus, "the incarnated essence of disorder" (22), a threat not only to personal peace, but also to the orderly give and take of civilized society. Given the chance, Peck spreads like a weed, secretly establishing a "University of Free Mind" with the provocative manifesto: "BE YOURSELF. GOOD IS THE SELF SPEAKING FREELY, EVIL IS WHAT PUTS THE SELF DOWN" (149). In contrast to Joe, Peck sees the social rather than the natural order as the major source of human misery. But these two intellectual adversaries respond to harsh realities in precisely the same way: both retreat.

A second intruder offers both Peck and Joe an impressive alternative to withdrawal. Marian Catlin, the pregnant young mother who moves into the empty house up the road, is a "biological perfectionist" in the philosophical tradition of Teilhard de Chardin. Marian does not deny the existence of personal pain and death, but she accepts them as essential elements in a larger, more beneficent framework. "What we call evil," she insists, "is only a groping toward good, part of the trial and error by which we move toward the perfected consciousness" (342). Naive, in clear violation of appearances, and utterly unverifiable, her philosophy is nevertheless one that produces positive human results. Marian is her own best argument. As Joe puts it, she is an irrepressible lover of all the little live things. She can summon up sympathy and affection for all forms of life, all varieties of experience. She can even accept the fact that she has been mutilated by cancer, that the cancer has recurred, and that her precious pregnancy will be a grim race between the forces of creation and destruction. Since Joe cannot face these cruel realities, he cannot provide Marian and her husband with the support they require. Joe consoles himself with the observation that he is at least more useful than Jim Peck. The guru of "the self speaking freely" is so self-absorbed that he fails to notice the crisis developing in his young neighbor's life.

What follows in *All the Little Live Things* is the chronicle of
Marian's decline and the painful intensification of Allston's impotent sympathy. The veteran Stegner reader will be reminded of
Elsa's slow death in *The Big Rock Candy Mountain.* And in Joe's
anguished reflections—his extrapolation from the cancerous disorder in Marian's body to the universal incoherence that threatens the
dignity of all life—he will recall similar thoughts in the mind of
Bruce Mason. Joe responds to Marian's exquisite vulnerability with
all the suppressed passion of a man who longed for daughters and
produced a single, ungrateful son. During the months of her suffering, he is totally preoccupied with the misfortunes of this comparative stranger; all of his thoughts and actions are colored by the
bitter consciousness of her impending death.

Thus when Tom Weld, the "native" owner of the Allston acres,
flattens an adjoining field for suburban subdivision, Joe reacts
with understandable but exaggerated fury: "I associated his mutilation of the hill with the mutilations that Marian had suffered and
was still to suffer, and I hated Weld so passionately that I
shook.... We could no more resist ... the Weldian notion that
mutilation was progress, than we could stop the malignant cells
from metastasizing through Marian's blood stream" (313). Similarly, when Julie LoPresti, another neighbor, punishes her parents
by allowing herself to become pregnant, Joe can summon little
sympathy. He is equally unmoved when the crisis finally transforms
the LoPrestis into his own ideal, a family with close personal ties:
"I could not forgive any of them for the fact that Julie's spite child
would be born and that Marian's love child had been a blob of blue
flesh that moved a little, and bleated weakly, and died" (344).
Finally, the catastrophe upsets Joe's uneasy truce with Jim Peck.
For nine months, as Peck's leafy hermitage develops into a
flourishing outpost of the University of the Free Mind, Allston
keeps his distance. Marian has faith in Peck, and Joe does not want
to disappoint her. But when the final confirmation of the girl's fate
coincides with the University of Free Mind's Fourth of July orgy,
Allston's self-control gives way. He banishes Comus and his crew
in a desperate, symbolic rejection of the disorder that is destroying
Marian.

The concluding scene of the novel suggests just how futile a gesture the banishment really is. In a climax almost too painful to
repeat, Stegner gathers all of his major characters together for a

final confrontation — Joe and Peck, Marian and her husband, Julie LoPresti, and Dave Weld, Tom's thoughtless son. Joe is driving Marian to the hospital. Death is very close. The bridge that serves as their only exit is blocked by the exiled Peck and his disgruntled disciples. Joe beeps his horn; an improbable assortment of vehicles roars to life; the LoPresti gelding panics and overturns Peck's motorcycle. When the smoke clears, the horse is down with two broken legs; one, a white peg of bone, is wedged in the rickety bridge that the Welds have neglected to repair. Marian's husband springs into action. He bludgeons the horse to death with merciful speed and clears the bridge, but he is not quick enough to spare his suffering wife the brutal spectacle. Marian's last glimpse of earth is a violent and ugly repudiation of her faith in "biological perfectionism," a gruesome tableau expressing "nature red of tooth and claw." At first, Joe lays the blame on Peck and his three cohorts. As he describes them, "Unthought, Irresponsibility, Rebellion, and Foolishness held a conference or a quarrel, and blocked the road" (331). But his fairer self soon reminds him that he shares their guilt; the carnage may have been precipitated by his own light taps on the horn. We are reminded of Joe's meditation on the slaughtered king snake: "Mischance is a collaboration . . . evil is everywhere and in all of us. . . . None of us, surely, is harmless, whatever our private fantasies urge us to believe" (92).

All the Little Live Things ends with a brief, beautiful, reflective epilogue that both confirms and corrects the sentiments expressed in the main body of the novel. Marian's tragedy is painful support for Joe's bleak assessment of the human condition. "God is kind?" he demands contemptuously. "Life is Good? Nature never did betray the heart that loved her? Then why the parting that she had? Why the reward she received for living intensely and generously and trying to die with dignity?" (342). At the conclusion of the novel, Joe finds "biological perfectionism" an even sillier and more sentimental philosophy than he did at the outset. Yet he cannot ignore its results in action. Marian's example has been an illuminating and influential one. Throughout her long ordeal, this naive girl maintained a graceful exterior of dignified self-control that Joe admires. He compares her courageous demeanor to that of a young queen bound for the scaffold. In the very worst of her pain, Marian found time and energy to assuage the sufferings of those around her. She gently detached herself from the affections of her six-year-old daughter and deliberately fostered a dependency upon the girl's father. In the same spirit, she arranged private conversations with Joe, conversations in which she attempted to console him with her own optimistic philosophy.

Joe remains unconvinced and unreconciled, but he is impressed with a compassion for others that persists through terrible pain and in the face of harsh death. The contrast with his earlier response to Curtis' demise is pointedly clear. Like his son, and like Jim Peck, his son's contemporary counterpart, Allston has settled his score with the world by withdrawing from it. His premature retirement is more conventional but no less irresponsible than Curtis' perpetual rebelliousness or Peck's mysticism. All three life-styles represent a retreat from things as they are; all three are cowardly; all three ignore the obligations of human brotherhood; and, finally, all three prove impossible to sustain, for, in Stegner's view, self-sufficiency is a childish illusion. Curtis dies young; Professor Peck is "busted" for taking on some under-age pupils; and Joe Allston is drawn back into this imperfect world by the potent innocence of Marian Catlin. Moreover, Allston's return will be a permanent one, for, like his predecessor Edwin Vickers, he has been forced to acknowledge the truth of MacLeish's verse: "Men are brothers by life lived and are hurt for it." The natural order may be brutal and absurd, but valiant resistance, not retreat, is the proper response. In the end, Joe has to account the pleasure of Marian's brief friendship well worth the agony of her loss. He concludes, "I shall be richer all my life for this sorrow" (345).

Joe Allston learns a great deal from Marian Catlin, despite their philosophical differences; on the other hand, he learns almost nothing from Jim Peck. One reviewer isolated this fact as the major defect in an otherwise convincing narrative.[4] We are inclined to disagree. A meliorist, Stegner maintains a limited faith in the individual's capacity for growth and development; he believes in "repair" but not in "conversion." In this light, Joe's antagonism to Peck's point of view is perfectly understandable. Generational and psychological conflicts combine to make the two men implacable adversaries. Indeed, their reconciliation would strike us as contrived and implausible.

Still, Joe's failure to reach an objective appraisal of Peck's "hippy" philosophy must be accounted a personal weakness. He is impatient and far from impartial. To put it another way, he is the possessor of serious, though hardly uncommon, human limitations. Paradoxically, Joe's personal shortcoming must be accounted the principal strength of *All the Little Live Things.* His running quarrel with Peck dramatizes that conflict between youth and age, optimism and skepticism, and between radical social and political values and their conservative counterparts that we have come across in several of Stegner's novels. We have seen Peck's kind before in Edwin Vickers and Paul Condon and Joe Hill, just as we have observed Joe Allston's qualities in Gustave Lund and Leonard MacDonald.

What we have not seen before is a treatment of the conflict in which the limitations of both sides are fully evident. Too often, especially in *On a Darkling Plain* and *Fire and Ice,* Stegner the moralist gets the best of Stegner the novelist; the right and the wrong are made improbably clear, and we come away with the strong suspicion that the deck has been loaded. In *All the Little Live Things,* on the other hand, Stegner dramatizes what we recognize as his own side of the quarrel in a narrator whose blind spots and prejudices are as manifest as the rightness of some of his opinions. Joe is much less patient than Lund, and less impeccably correct than MacDonald, and for all that more recognizably human. In his obvious shortcomings he is more fully a part of the imperfect world that he surveys than his fictional predecessors. He is, we feel, one of us. More than a purveyor of right opinions, Joe is a fully realized personality. We may catch echoes of Wallace Stegner in what he has to say, but the voice we hear is Joe Allston's.

IV Angle of Repose

Wallace Stegner found the raw materials for his tenth novel in an authentic chapter of Western history. *Angle of Repose,* a complex, ambitious work that spans four generations and a continent, has as its focus the fictionalized biography of the turn-of-the-century writer and illustrator, Mary Hallock Foote (1847–1938). Largely neglected since World War I, Mrs. Foote's life and work have recently attracted critical attention. Before we turn to Stegner's imaginative reconstruction of her life, it will be useful to examine the objectively verifiable events of her long career.[5]

Born in upstate New York in 1847, Mary Haviland Hallock enjoyed the mixed blessings of a nineteenth-century rural girlhood.

By her own account, her father "belonged to the last of his breed of thinking and reading American farmers" (5). Jeffersonian yeomen and schismatic Quakers, the Hallocks were high-minded, hard-working, and perpetually impoverished. The much-indulged baby of the family, "Molly" readily persuaded her parents to let her pursue an enthusiasm for drawing. In 1864 she entered the Cooper Union School of Design, the only such program open to women in the city of New York. Her Cooper Union years provided the young artist with valuable social and professional contacts as well as with competent instruction. By the early 1870s, Molly was illustrating the works of such luminaries as Henry Wadsworth Longfellow and John Greenleaf Whittier. She had also formed what was to be a lifelong friendship with Helena de Kay, a glamorous New York aristocrat and the wife of Richard Watson Gilder, the foremost American literary editor of his day. In view of her obscure beginnings and the rigid conventions that governed the lives of Victorian gentlewomen, Mary Hallock achieved extraordinary success in the genteel world of Eastern art before her marriage exiled her forever to the West. After 1876 this cultivated New Yorker reluctantly made her home in the mining camps and on the irrigation projects of Idaho, Colorado, and California. She is remembered today as a meticulous chronicler of the last American frontier.

Mary's husband, Arthur De Wint Foote, was a talented and idealistic scientist-pioneer. The son of a New England country squire, Foote spent two years at Yale's Sheffield Scientific School until eye trouble interrupted his studies in 1868. Thereafter, as a self-educated junior engineer, he depended upon his rather uneven native abilities for advancement. Honest, energetic, and mechanically inventive, Foote displayed extraordinary tact with "machines, human subordinates, and work animals" (10). During his fifty-year career he made (and neglected to patent) several important contributions to engineering science. He also developed a reputation for consistent fairness with his employees. Partners and superiors, however, presented this upright young engineer with serious problems. Most of his mining and irrigation projects were dependent on outside investors. Foote disliked submitting to their authority, especially when they required him to subordinate the rigorous demands of science to the profit motive. Self-righteous and something of a snob, he alternately trusted his investors too much or too little. In either case, the result was financial disaster.

For the first two decades of her married life—what she called "the restless years" (4)—the West meant more than cultural poverty to Mary Hallock Foote.

Arthur's work first took the young couple to New Almaden, California, one of the world's most productive quicksilver mines. Their brief sojourn there brought Molly both a child and a new career. Intrigued by her vivid letters, the Gilders commissioned descriptive essays and short stories of the "local color" variety then in vogue. Thereafter, the young artist enjoyed equal success as a writer and illustrator of fiction. After a short, enforced vacation in nearby Santa Cruz, Arthur found a second job in the Rocky Mountain boom town of Leadville, Colorado. Perhaps the most exciting mining camp of its day, Leadville attracted a glittering crowd of what Molly termed "professional exiles" (13): well-born and well-educated Easterners, such as her husband, whose work required them to live on the outskirts of civilized society. From 1879 to 1880, the Footes hosted a veritable salon of distinguished intellectuals, including Clarence King, the first director of the United States Geological Survey, and fellow author and reformer, Helen Hunt Jackson. Molly delighted in this improbable Western re-creation of the New York cultural world. Leadville's professional exiles inspired her first novel; they also provided the cast of characters for most of her important later work.

Their Leadville vein played out, the Footes next embarked for the silver mines of Michoacán, Mexico. Their visit was brief, but Molly was deeply impressed by the graceful elegance of the "medieval" culture. A happy interlude of sheer "romance" (209), the Footes' Mexican adventure was succeeded by eleven years of personal and financial disaster. In 1884, Arthur moved the family to Idaho and attempted to form an irrigation company in the rich but arid Boise River Valley. His was a bright idea that was simply ahead of its time. The slow collapse of his irrigation project ruined Foote financially, turned him into a drinker, and threatened to destroy his marriage. His artistic wife, never an enthusiastic Westerner, found Idaho a social and cultural wasteland. Tied to a man she had come to regard as a stubborn, impractical dreamer, Molly attempted a trial separation in 1889. After a few lonely weeks in British Columbia, she returned to Boise, "irrevocably committed to the part of an anxious wife" (35). For the duration of the "restless years," however, her articles and illustrations supplied the bulk of the Foote family's income.

In 1895, Arthur finally found a position commensurate with his peculiar talents. As manager of the North Star gold mine in Grass Valley, California, he achieved financial security and at the same time retained the freedom to design equipment and direct his immediate staff. Foote ran the North Star with skill and tact until his retirement from engineering. The three and a half decades at Grass Valley were fulfilling years for husband and wife alike. In 1896, Molly refused the principalship of Cooper Union, fearful of "failure from the foundation, failure to 'stick together'" (390); but she continued to write and publish until the demand for "local colorists" finally subsided.

Only one unhappy incident upset the even tenor of the North Star years. In 1904 death claimed their beloved twenty-year-old daughter Agnes, the brightest product of the Idaho debacle. Aside from that tragedy, their Grass Valley years brought this hard-working couple to "the angle of repose" — the slope at which rocks cease to fall — a geological term which Molly always thought "too good to waste on rockslides or heaps of sand" (306).

In retrospect it is easy to guess why the Foote family history caught Stegner's eye. On one level, Molly Foote was faced with the problems of a typical Western homemaker; above all, she was determined to bring civilization to the raw frontier. On another level, she was a nineteenth-century Eastern artist, independent, ambitious, genteel, and apt to confuse fine words with great deeds. Her husband Arthur, on the other hand, was a fully committed Western pioneer. Like his occasional employer, John Wesley Powell, Foote combined the informed pragmatism of a trained scientist with the idealism and energy of a visionary; unlike Powell, however, he was arrogant, rigid, and unwilling to compromise. In brief, the Footes repeat the familiar polarities we have already encountered in Bo and Elsa Mason — male and female, wanderer and nester, dreamer and realist. Moreover, they embody these dichotomies in a more complex and ultimately more interesting form. Both Arthur and Molly were strong-willed, tough-minded individualists; both were important Western builders; both displayed serious lapses of judgment. While they engage Stegner's sympathy, neither invites the kind of sentimental portrayal that distorts Elsa Mason and upsets the aesthetic balance of *The Big Rock Candy Mountain.*

Stegner's account of the actual genesis of *Angle of Repose* confirms our speculations. He explained, in an interview with us, that

Mary Hallock Foote first attracted his attention in the late 1940s. Impressed with the authentic Western detail recorded by this literary gentlewoman, Stegner took notice of her work in a lecture course on American realism. Shortly thereafter, he acquired five hundred letters and a typescript version of her unpublished reminiscences for the Stanford University Library, where they rested undisturbed for over twenty years. In the late 1960s, Stegner finally returned to the neglected Foote papers. A cursory examination revealed that Arthur De Wint Foote was as interesting a psychological and historical type as his more distinguished wife. Still, it was the interaction between the pair that most stimulated his imagination. Stegner immediately decided "there must be a book somewhere in there"; deciding what kind of book it should be took more time. First he contemplated a full-scale biography. Before long, however, he recognized that neither of the Footes had achieved enough to merit such formal and scholarly treatment. He next considered making them the protagonists in a conventional historical novel, a "costume drama" laid entirely in the Victorian period; but he rejected this alternative on the grounds that "the only real use for the past was to find the present in the past and the past in the present and let them feed back and forth." In the end, and scarcely to our surprise, Stegner decided to incorporate the Foote saga into a novel of "the middle ground," one that would change or supplement historical — in this case biographical — fact, in the interests of discovering and dramatizing continuities between past and present. Most crucially, Stegner needed a "present" to relate to the Foote past, and a narrator to stand between him and his fictionalized reconstruction of the family history. He found both in Lyman Ward, the imaginary grandson he created for Mary Hallock Foote.

Lyman Ward is reared by his grandparents, Oliver and Susan Burling Ward (the fictional equivalents of Arthur and Mary Hallock Foote) amid the peace and security of their Grass Valley refuge. Deeply impressed by his grandparents' mutual respect and support, young Lyman has little reason to doubt the stability of their "angle of repose." His is a quiet, contented, rather studious childhood. As a young adult, he makes effortless progress from the graduate history program at Harvard University to a teaching post at the University of Wisconsin. He reads, publishes, wins the prestigious Bancroft prize, and gradually earns the respect of his colleagues. He also marries Ellen Hammond — "a reader, a walker, a rather *still* woman"[6] — and fathers a son, Rodman. After a stretch at Dartmouth, Lyman returns with his small family to California and to a full professorship at the Berkeley campus of the state university.

As Lyman enters middle age, however, his orderly progress from one success to another begins to falter. Rodman is very much his own man, and a disappointment to his father. With ill-disguised scorn for history, Rodman earns higher degrees in sociology — in Lyman's view, a dangerous pseudoscience which reduces "change" to "process," "values" to "data," and dismisses all evidence "more than ten years" old as out of date (18). Moreover, Rodman is what his father abhors, an idealistic radical full of contempt for the Christian-capitalist ethos. The past, in Rodman's reckoning, is a chronicle of corruption unworthy of his concern; the "now" is all. As the result of their total disagreement over the value of history, Lyman and his son have strong differences on almost every important issue. As Lyman puts it, "that is no gap between the generations, that is a gulf" (17).

Rodman's defection is only the beginning. In the midst of heated ideological quarrels, Lyman is struck by a painful and progressive arthritic condition. The disease calcifies his skeleton, fuses his neck to the top of his spine, and makes a grotesque creature of him — "Gorgon," "Man of Stone," "Nemesis in a wheelchair." It costs him a leg and, subsequently, his wife. While Lyman recuperates from the amputation, Ellen runs off with his surgeon. Her betrayal is as unexpected as her motives are obscure. Was it "calculation," "intolerable pity," or simply "an unseemly post-menopausal itch" (443)? Lyman cannot guess. In any case, he is unwilling to forgive her, despite the fact that her "surgical playmate" (442) is dead and that she and Rodman are eager for reconciliation. Embittered, rigid in mind and body, with an uncertain future and a past in need of reappraisal, Lyman retires to Grass Valley to write a biography of his grandparents. His rationale is apparently simple. "I'd like to live in their clothes a while, if only so I don't have to live in my own" (17). Whether he knows it or not, Lyman's retreat into the past will take him to the center of "the middle ground."

Lyman quickly completes the preparations for his review of family history. He adapts his grandparents' old cottage to the needs of a wheelchair-bound tenant, assembles the relevant papers, and hires a local girl to help him file and transcribe. His assistant, Shelly Hawkes, a fourth-generation Grass Valley resident, has a personal stake in the projected biography. Both her father and grandfather assisted Oliver Ward at the North Star mine; her mother, Lyman's childhood playmate, now serves as his nurse. More important, Shelly is a Berkeley dropout who shares the contempt for the past displayed by Lyman's son. Like young Rodman, she looks forward to a dramatic revolution in social and political institutions; but, where Rodman favors the notion of a scientifically organized Utopia, Shelly envisions a future society that is "natural," anarchistic, and effortlessly just. Following the lead of her shaggy boyfriend, Larry Rasmussen, she advocates a rural, communal experiment not unlike Jim Peck's Free University. Outspoken, inquisitive, and distressingly provocative, Shelly is hardly the ideal companion for Lyman's excursion into the past.

Speaking extemporaneously into a tape recorder, Lyman opens the family chronicle with a free-wheeling review of his grandmother's courtship and marriage. In a manner reminiscent of his treatment of Joe Hill, Stegner, through his narrator, relates the "what" of the story with as much fidelity to historical fact as the record permits; in fact, the details of Lyman's narrative differ little from the actual experiences of Mary Hallock Foote. Susan Burling meets Oliver Ward at a New York soiree, corresponds with him for five years while he establishes himself in the West, and marries him in simple Quaker fashion. The "why" of the story, however, is a different matter. Even for a Victorian memoir, Mrs. Foote's reminiscences are strangely silent in the area of motives. The silence is at once suggestive and tempting. What went on in the mind of this elusive woman? What drew her to an uncultivated engineer like Arthur De Wint Foote? Had Stegner chosen to proceed solely as an historian, he would have had to bypass these intriguing questions. As a novelist of "the middle ground," however, he is free, even obliged, to extrapolate and invent. His narrator Lyman consciously violates the rules of historical evidence when he sifts through his grandmother's papers for psychological clues. Gathering his findings together, he arrives at a plausible but utterly unverifiable explanation for the engagement and subsequent marriage.

According to Lyman, Augusta Drake and Thomas Hudson (the fictional equivalents of Helena de Kay and Richard Watson Gilder) are the original objects of Susan Burling's affection. Augusta, a

bold, dark beauty, excites admiration and perhaps passion as well
— Lyman is shocked by "the suggestion of lesbianism" (34) in
their early correspondence. Thomas represents Susan's *beau ideal*
— he is "gentility personified, sensibility made flesh" (54). When
Thomas and Augusta marry, Susan is excluded and hurt; but,
making the best of a difficult situation, she turns to her faithful
Western correspondent and "reserve possibility" (53), Oliver
Ward. She finds herself drawn to Oliver's integrity, virility, and
physical competence; at the same time, she is dismayed by his social
ineptitude and ignorance of the arts. At the time of their marriage
her ambivalence remains unresolved. Lyman, who is naturally a bit
tender on the score of marital infidelity, views his grandmother's
irresolution as a grave disloyalty and as the key to her subsequent
failings as Oliver's mate.

Satisfied with this reconstruction of his grandparents' courtship,
Lyman turns to the first two decades of their married life: the years
in New Almaden, Leadville, Michoacán, and Idaho. Once again,
the facts of his narrative duplicate what we know to have been the
actual experiences of Mary Hallock Foote. However, Stegner
makes several critical departures from the historical record.
Reasonable extrapolations, they nevertheless amount to an interpretation, rather than a mere recounting, of the story. Through
Lyman, Stegner returns to the elusive "why."

According to her reminiscences, Mrs. Foote's beloved band of
"professional exiles" included an extraordinary number of
romantic young men. Steve Fleming staved off claim jumpers with
a "comprehensive" (205) Winchester; Ferdinand Van Zandt
lynched a murderer, married an heiress, then took his own life —
"blown out like an unspent torch in a blast of wind" (253); the
"susceptible" (268) Harry Tompkins bound volumes of Wordsworth "in cream white lambskin with robin's-egg-blue paper
lining" (296). Stegner compresses these colorful youngsters — so
different from the stolid Arthur Foote — into the single character
Frank Sargent. More important, Stegner expands their affectionate
regard for Molly into a full-blooded passion.

As Lyman reconstructs the affair, Frank, who is Oliver's trusted
assistant, falls in love with Susan during the Leadville period.
Susan pretends to dismiss his regard as an insignificant "school-
boy" attachment. In reality, however, her imperfect respect for
Oliver makes her dangerously susceptible to Frank's social and cul-

tural graces. The barren Idaho years finally bring her disloyalty to a fruition far more terrible than mere infidelity. As Oliver's irrigation scheme enters into final decline, Frank and Susan, under the pretext of taking five-year-old Agnes Ward for a walk, steal away into the privacy of the countryside. The adults sink deep into talk; the child slips away unnoticed; a few hours later, Agnes' body is found floating in a nearby canal. Frank Sargent commits suicide the day after her funeral. A trusting man whose trust has been violated, the grief-stricken Oliver assumes the worst and makes the break that his wife often contemplated but never accomplished. The Wards live apart for two years until family and friends force a reconciliation. For the remaining half century of their marriage, Oliver treats Susan "with a sort of grave infallible kindness" (562); but, as Lyman puts it, "he never forgave her.... She broke something she couldn't mend" (563).

Wallace Stegner has explained that he made Lyman Ward an historian because he wanted "to preach through him." Sociologists like Rodman, he said, and dropouts like Shelly, have turned their backs on the past in the foolish assurance that the present and future can be rapidly made over into something different and far better. To a degree the novel reflects Stegner's determination to preach. Most readers will recognize that Lyman shares important attitudes with his creator: "Quiet desperation is another name for the human condition" (519); "Civilizations grow and change and decline — they aren't remade" (519). The fact remains, however, that we feel less preached at in *Angle of Repose* than in any of Stegner's earlier novels. Like Joe Allston in *All the Little Live Things,* perhaps even more so, Lyman is a fully conceived, fully developed, perfectly plausible human being. We are persuaded that his opinions — along with his gruffness and skepticism — are integral to his character; they flow naturally from what he fundamentally is. Paradoxically, then, Stegner has at once written himself into and out of his narrator. That paradox is one important element in the success of *Angle of Repose.*

It may be that the paradox goes deeper still. Throughout this novel there runs the illusion that the author is Lyman Ward, not Wallace Stegner. At one point Lyman reflects on possible titles for his book. Appropriately enough, he comes up with *Angle of Repose.* But, if Lyman does what Stegner does, then he does it with a difference. At the outset Lyman looks to the past not in order to discover continuities; rather, betrayed by his son and abandoned by his wife, he goes to the past — specifically, to his grandparents — assured that it is quite unlike the present. "This present of 1970," he feels, "is no more an extension of my grandparents' world, this West is no more a development of the West they helped build, than the sea over Santorin is an extension of that once-island of rock and olives" (18). No less than Rodman and Shelly, Lyman finds the present unacceptable. Like them again, he sets out after something better on the assumption that past and present are discontinuous. If Lyman Ward, eminent historian, is correct in his assumption, then there is no "middle ground" to strive for, no connections to be made. He must learn how wrong he is.

At a rather late moment in his story Lyman continues to describe himself as "Coe Professor of History, Emeritus, living a day in his grandparents' life to avoid paying too much attention to his own" (409). From the beginning he has admitted that his flight to the past is actually a flight from the present. What he has not yet seen is that his flight is utterly futile; or, to put it another way, that thinking on his family history will lead him right back to himself. He begins to glimpse this truth when he reopens the question of his motives for pursuing his grandparents: "Is it love and sympathy that makes me think myself capable of reconstructing these lives, or am I, Nemesis in a wheelchair, bent on proving something — perhaps that not even gentility and integrity are proof against the corrosions of human weakness, human treachery, human disappointment, human inability to forget?" (439).

As Lyman approaches the full revelation of his grandmother's infidelity, he begins to recoil. History, this idyl of imagined serenity, begins to look shockingly like the present. Can it be that Susan Ward was an adultress? "I cannot imagine it, I say. I do not believe it. Yet I have seen the similar breakdown of one whose breakdown I couldn't possibly have imagined until it happened, whose temptations I was not even aware of" (508). Fuller knowledge of Oliver's reaction to Susan's betrayal is equally difficult to accept; for Oliver, upon learning of his wife's infidelity and his daughter's drowning, returns to the bleak mesa that is the site of their Idaho home. As Susan watches from a window, he slowly, methodically rips up the dozens of rose bushes that he had planted for his wife. These, the eloquent symbols of his love and trust, he destroys. Nearly two years later, when the family is finally reunited, it is clear that those flowers will never bloom again. Reluctantly, Lyman acknowledges that what he had imagined to be a stable "angle of repose" was nothing more than a cold, joyless standoff. Far from a consoling alternative, the past turns out to be a painful prefiguring of the present. Just as surely as the "human weakness" of Susan Ward anticipates the frailty of Ellen Ward, Oliver's "inability to forget" looks ahead to the same response in his grandson. We are not altogether surprised when Lyman decides "there is some history that I want not to have happened" (512).

The full implications of his family history only gradually reach the surface of Lyman's consciousness. As we have seen, his first reaction is disbelief. Later, once he has absorbed the grave details of his reconstruction, he casts his eye back over the protagonists, his grandparents. To his grandmother, whom he once loved because he imagined her perfect, he now brings more complex and more durable sentiments. To love he adds compassion and respect for the strength of her character. Susan Ward "was a perfect lady, and a lady who was a feeling, eager, talented, proud, snobbish, an exiled woman. And fallible. And responsible, willing to accept the blame for her actions. . . . She held herself to account, and she was terribly punished" (534). His grandfather survives in his mind as the fairest, most trusting man he ever knew. Oliver Ward made you feel safe. There is but one diminishing qualification. Lyman has "difficulty justifying that bleak and wordless break, and that ripping-up of the rose garden, that was vindictive and pitiless. I wish he had not done that. I think he never got over being ashamed, and never found the words to say so" (540).

It would be misleading to say that Lyman learns from the chronicle of betrayal and grief that he has uncovered. Rather, he is impelled by it. Learning would involve the conscious admission that the words "vindictive and pitiless" apply to him almost as well as they do to his grandfather. Such an admission would not come easily to a man who has been deserted and whose mind and emotions are as frozen as his body. On the other hand, such a man might recognize the truth about himself if it revealed itself first to his unconscious. With something like this in mind, and in a moment of remarkable psychological acuity, Stegner decided to conclude *Angle of Repose* with a dream.

Ellen arrives at the cottage. She does not say so, but it is obvious that she has come to appeal for reconciliation. Helpless in his chair, brimming with resentment, Lyman feels pursued. He is distant, evasive, vaguely fearful that she will request what his grandmother mutely requested in 1890 — that her wronged husband forgive and forget. Ellen asks, "What do you mean, 'Angle of Repose'?" Lyman replies, "Horizontal. Permanently." Ellen "moved her shoulders, half turned, looked at me and away. Talking to Grandmother's portrait she said, 'Death? Living death? Fifty years of it? No rest till they lay down? There must be something . . . short of that. She couldn't have been doing penance for fifty years'" (561–62). The drift of Lyman's dream work — that the "inability to forget" a violation of trust destroys what remains valuable in life — brings the crucial issue into clear focus. Should he reject Ellen's appeal, should he be as cold and intractable as Oliver was, he will condemn himself and his wife to living death. It is with horror and pity that he remembers his grandparents' bitter truce: "In all the years I lived with them I never saw them kiss, I never saw them put their arms around each other, I never saw them touch!" (563). The dream ends in a kind of erotic catharsis. Lyman's simultaneous terror and sexual excitement function as the unconscious correlatives to his waking shame at his physical deformity and the attendant repression of libido. Having faced what he feared in his grandparents, he must face what he fears in himself. At the end of the nightmare, we feel, lies renewed humanity.

As he awakens from his dream, Lyman is aware that his dream "represents some occult truth about *me*" (567). Lyman is not an optimist. Personal experience has confirmed his somber view of the human condition. Ironically, his investigation of his grandparents, an enterprise grounded in the assumption that life was purer and simpler in days gone by, works to the same effect. At the end of the novel the net result of Lyman's recent experience is a revision and a question. Angle of repose, he decides, is a too sanguine description of what most couples can achieve. As Lyman construes it, an "intersection of lines" is much less optimistic but for that reason probably a more accurate metaphor: "Some cowardly, hopeful geometer in my brain tells me it is the angle at which two lines prop each other up, the leaning-together from the vertical which produces the false arch. For lack of a keystone, the false arch may be as much as one can expect in this life." The question is whether or not Lyman and Ellen will be able to form such an arch. "I lie wondering," he closes, "if I am man enough to be a bigger man than my grandfather" (569).

Lyman's discovery of continuities between past and present is at once dismaying and affirmative. On the dark side is the revelation that the constants in history are hardship, betrayal, and bitter suffering. Paradoxically, one of the lessons of the past is that our false arches will stand only if we learn to forget. Lyman is a better man for having reviewed the lives of Oliver and Susan Ward. That is affirmative. To be our best, Stegner has suggested more than once, we must know the worst. *Angle of Repose* is his most eloquent and comprehensive articulation of that theme. Through the imaginative rendering of Western persons, places, and events, the novel unveils continuities between past and present and thereby arrives at "the middle ground." And it does more. By dramatizing the process of discovery in the consciousness of Lyman Ward, *Angle of Repose* illustrates both the operation and the profound significance of historical continuities in human experience. Lyman's exploration of the past causes him great pain, but it also brings him back, enlightened and enriched, to himself.

CHAPTER 6

Epilogue

WE began by tracing the margins of the Stegner country; we must conclude by placing Stegner in the tradition of the American novel. To a remarkable degree, the geographic and literary places overlap. True, Stegner is a distant literary relative of William Dean Howells, one of the earliest defenders of American realism. True again, at certain moments — in *On a Darkling Plain,* for example — his work is dimly reminiscent of earlier American experiments with naturalism. One realizes almost immediately, however, that the defining characteristics of Stegner's art are neither stylistic, though his style is distinctive, and tends to be "realistic," nor philosophical, though he possesses strong views on human nature and morality. Rather, it is region and personal experience within that region that have been the crucial determinants in the development of his art. The best of his narratives, his most persistent themes, his direct, muscular style, his philosophical views — all take life from the memory of formative events in a very specific landscape. It is therefore truest to say that Stegner belongs to that large family of American writers whose works have been defined by region. Edward Eggleston and Sarah Orne Jewett come to mind. So, in their different ways, do Jack London, Frank Norris, Hamlin Garland, Sherwood Anderson, Sinclair Lewis, the early John Steinbeck, and Stegner's own model writer of "the middle ground," William Faulkner. At the head of the family, of course, stands Mark Twain.

Mark Twain's impact on American fiction has been so sweeping and so widely acknowledged that the discovery of his influence on an individual writer is rarely much of a surprise. Still, while they are more or less obvious, the similarities between Stegner and Mark Twain are noteworthy. For both, childhood on the margins of civilization formed the basis in experience for subsequent art. For both, too, the pull of larger cultural centers resulted in flight from the West, but also meant divided allegiances and personal restlessness (a restlessness which turns up as a dominant theme in their work). Their ransacking of memory — the full submission to an imaginative counterpull back to a special place and to the unforgettable time of boyhood — followed upon their achievement of adulthood and the decision to become a writer. If East End, Saskatchewan, is Stegner's Hannibal, then *The Big Rock Candy Mountain* is his *Huckleberry Finn* and *Wolf Willow* his *Life on the Mississippi.*

The autobiographical impulse leads, for both writers, to explorations of youth, innocence, initiation, and disillusionment. The fact that they resolved such questions in rather different ways — Stegner is not inclined, as Mark Twain was, to damn the *entire* human race — should serve as a reminder that there is much these writers do not share. Most notably, Stegner has displayed little interest in regional dialect, is rather slenderly gifted as a humorist, and seems well insulated against the nihilism and solipsism which poisoned Mark Twain's later life. Mark Twain, on the other hand, though obsessed with the past, wrote nothing that we can place beside Stegner's contributions to historiography. At a more general level, this brief comparison illustrates that the significant similarities between Mark Twain and Wallace Stegner are predominantly cultural in origin — both display characteristically American patterns of artistic response to distinctively American experiences — while the important differences can be traced to personal predilection and individual talent. In short, then, Mark Twain is the grand progenitor of the broad native tradition in which Stegner has worked.

We can draw much tighter and more direct lines of kinship between Stegner and his closest regional and literary cousins, Bernard DeVoto and Willa Cather. In his *The Uneasy Chair: A Biography of Bernard DeVoto,* Stegner readily acknowledges the parallels between his own career and his subject's.

First by accident and later through his friendship and example, the curve of my life has touched some of the points that Bernard DeVoto's did. We were both boys in Utah, though at different times and in different towns. We were both Westerners by birth and upbringing, novelists by intention, teachers by necessity, and historians by the sheer compulsion of the region that shaped us. We both made our way eastward to Harvard, with a stop in the Middle West. We were for some years neighbors in Cambridge and colleagues at the Bread Loaf Writers' Conference. The same compulsion that made amateur historians of us made us conservationists as well.... But until I began this biography I had not realized how many of my basic attitudes about the West, about America in general, about literature, and about history parallel his, either because so much of our experience retraced the same curve or because of his direct influence.[1]

As the friend, and in some respects the protégé of DeVoto, Stegner might have made *The Uneasy Chair* an exercise in hagiography, making war on common enemies and old detractors. Happily. he does not. The biography succeeds admirably in achieving its stated objective: "to re-create Benny DeVoto as he was — flawed, brilliant, provocative, outrageous, running scared all his life, often wrong, often spectacularly right, always stimulating, sometimes infuriating, and never, never dull" (ix–x).

True to the man it portrays, *The Uneasy Chair* is itself never dull. Much of its energy springs naturally from its subject, Bernard DeVoto, whose impact upon American intellectual life during the decades before his death in 1955 might be measured best in seismic units. Whether he was attacking (and he was always attacking) Van Wyck Brooks and the Eastern literary establishment, or Western landgrabbers, or Senator Joseph McCarthy, or the Federal Bureau of Investigation, he did so with gusto, vehemence, even an anger so nearly excessive as to seem the symptom of a deeper defensiveness. At root, Stegner persuades us, DeVoto was a kind of regional hybrid of Eastern and Western values, aspirations, histories, and styles. At first, DeVoto was a disaffected Westerner in flight from the culturally impoverished provinces. Later, at Harvard, feeling himself on the margins of the culture and the community, he became rather boisterously the Westerner. This gap in his identity, which never completely closed, bore with it both constructive and destructive potentials. On one hand, regional cross-fertilization produced vigor and tenacity and originality, qualities which flourished in DeVoto's massive trilogy on the American West — *The Year of Decision: 1846* (1943), *Across the Wide Missouri* (1948), *The Course of Empire* (1952). On the other, it fostered conflict, a neurotic need for overwork, and the anger and defensiveness that bedevil the outsider.

Another, perhaps less evident, source of energy in *The Uneasy Chair* is the confident penetration of Stegner's analysis. Confidence and insight are, in turn, rooted in numerous affinities between author and subject. Some of these, as we have noted, Stegner acknowledges — common experiences in similar places, and similar careers in shared disciplines. Other affinities appear in the biography in lower relief, but in the aggregate they amount to a profile of attitudes and values common to Stegner and DeVoto. While he is always commendably detached and objective, it is nonetheless fair to say that Stegner discovered the rough outlines of himself in *The Uneasy Chair.*

Childhood and adolescence in a remote Western province is, of course, the common point of departure. It was in Utah, Stegner argues, that DeVoto first developed a "sense that culture existed only farther east and among people of another kind, and a pronounced, forced-draft hunger for the intellectual life" (5). The point is true to the facts of DeVoto's life, and those facts of life find confirmation in Stegner's own experience. In the East, at Harvard, but more especially in Vermont, DeVoto discovered his own ideal of America.

Every quality of independence, self-reliance, laboriousness, ingenuity, stubbornness, endurance, and hard-mouthed integrity that DeVoto admired in the New England character were here undiluted. Town-meeting democracy, democratic self-respect, an essential conservatism that went all the way from frugality in making things do, and do again, and do over, to a skeptical and humorous political view were demonstrated to him twenty times a day. (102)

A few years later, in the same place, Stegner found the same ideal. In a recent interview with us, he described himself as a Westerner, but reserved Vermont as the one Eastern place where he feels at home: "the state is essentially frontier, and most of the frontier virtues and a lot of the frontier handicrafts and handinesses still persist. Life is a little closer to the bone, with less fat on it and less smog around it, in Vermont."[2]

For both Stegner and DeVoto, the flight East involved the discovery of a rural culture which provided them with a kind of home, but which also, ironically, forced them to reassess the Western home from which they had come. In the short run, this turnabout led to a more positive evaluation of the region they had abandoned, especially in its frontier phase. In robust Rocky Mountain trappers, in explorers, in hardy pioneers, for Stegner in the Mormons, the virtues of the Vermont yeoman found Western expression. In the long run, however, the backward view enforced a more somber interpretation of developments in America since the closing of the frontier. The Western failure to preserve and build upon the frontier ideal had its parallel, at a further stage of development, in the urban Northeast. Industrialization, urban- and suburbanization, rapacious consumption of natural resources, along with the other political and social ills of twentieth-century America, were as surely a part of the Western future as they were of the Eastern past. According to Stegner, even that once ideal pocket of New England is not exempt: "Vermont is obviously on its way to becoming another New Hampshire, which is to say a suburb of Boston and Montreal."[3] In the face of what seemed inevitable and inevitably unpleasant, DeVoto was not optimistic: "America was potentially a great place, but it was lousy with Americans" (361). Twenty years later, his biographer is of like mind: "I don't think any part of America is going to escape the Americans."[4]

But Vermont provided more than somber American perspectives in the 1930s. Most crucially, it provided the annual Bread Loaf Writers' Conference, where both DeVoto and Stegner, errant, self-conscious Westerners, felt like (and were) "insiders" in a congenial Eastern setting. While open to a variety of literary viewpoints, the emphasis at the Conference "was practical and professional" (126). With DeVoto as one of its principal designers and exponents, "the Bread Loaf teaching was a how-to course — how to do, how to avoid." "Inevitably," Stegner goes on, it reflected DeVoto's attitudes,

and it helped to establish Bread Loaf as a hard-headed, commonsensical, practical academy, anti-faddist, anti-modernist, anti-Bohemian, anti-Marxist, anti-coterie ... more inclined to stress the traditional than the experimental or revolutionary. And, DeVoto might have added, more inclined to think than to throb, more inclined to consult fact and experience than wishful theory, more interested in communication than in self-expression, exhibitionism, or public confession. (128)

Here, no doubt partly in response to his own literary instincts, but certainly under DeVoto's influence, Stegner developed the practical attitude toward the business of writing that has been a conspicuous feature of his career ever since.

Vermont also provided Robert Frost, the *genius loci* of Bread Loaf, and a man who agreed with DeVoto on the essential dignity of the yeoman farmer who survived on ingenuity, determination, and three hundred dollars a year. As an adjunct to this shared ideal, Frost reinforced DeVoto's hostility to "aesthetes and Capital-A Artists, thinkers of beautiful thoughts, abstract theorizers, and writers of cherished prose" (79). Political, social, and artistic in implication, this cluster or related attitudes has had obvious impact in Stegner's scheme of values. We have mentioned his frank literary professionalism. We can add, without exhausting the evidence, his critical view of Marxism in *Fire and Ice;* Joe Allston's rejection of the "Glandular Genius" in "Field Guide to the Western Birds"; Joe's equally angry rejection of "youth culture," communes, and utopian schemes in *All the Little Live Things;* and Lyman Ward's contempt for sociological abstractions in *Angle of Repose.* At the core of this persistent pattern of criticism is the conviction, shared by DeVoto and Stegner, that romantic literary posturings, like theoretical programs for rapid social reform, are the products of ignorance and the perverse unwillingness to face and accept things as they are. In this light, one of Stegner's concluding descriptions of DeVoto — "He was a middlist, or an equilibrist. He suspected extremes, and he had a passionate faith in common sense" (356) — applies with almost equal accuracy to himself.

Although this marshaling of personal affinities could be materially extended, perhaps we have said enough to suggest the close connections, personal and intellectual, between Stegner and his subject in *The Uneasy Chair.* The book is at once a valuable record, a tribute, and an indirect statement of its author's attitudes and values. Having said this much, it is equally important that Stegner is willing to be bluntly candid about DeVoto's personal shortcomings and professional limitations. More than once, for example, he notes that DeVoto's irascibility, and his penchant for vituperation and overstatement, worked to weaken what were otherwise perfectly defensible positions. When his involvement in issues was deeply personal, as it usually was, DeVoto had a way of pushing too hard. As the reflex of his defensiveness, he anticipated, and therefore often precipitated, hostile responses. As Stegner puts it, "his material twisted in his hands when he himself was part of it, and his reporting acquired the tones of grievance and denunciation" (66).

Perhaps as a kind of corrective, DeVoto believed that as a fiction writer he should confine himself to third person narration. Functioning as a kind of gag on the author, the third person narrator

was obliged, according to DeVoto, to keep his opinions, his speculations, his confessions, to himself. Ironically, this corrective
failed, for it required of DeVoto that he become a ventriloquist, an
artist who remains invisible while projecting his views into the
minds and through the mouths of his characters.

A weakness in DeVoto as a novelist was that he never mastered ventriloquism.... DeVoto was a man full of opinions. He marshaled facts with
great swiftness and made them into generalizations, and he discriminated
among ideas with the positiveness of one discriminating between sound
and rotten oranges. The iconic and hesitant representation of ideas as
people was not enough for him. When he couldn't judge and comment, he
was inhibited; when he couldn't speak in his own voice, he was
constrained. (243)

Whatever the liabilities of speaking *in propria persona,* it was impossible for DeVoto to mute his own voice, and therefore impossible for him to write completely successful fiction in the third
person. This was an artistic weakness, to be sure, but it had the
important compensation that DeVoto's strong, independent, opinionated voice provides the energy and excitement in the best of his
work as an historian. In discovering, reluctantly, perhaps never
completely, that he was not a novelist, DeVoto also discovered that
he was at his best when setting forth the dramatic narrative of the
American West.

Where DeVoto failed to refine the art of ventriloquism, Stegner,
most notably in the last decade, has succeeded. In fact, his focusing
on DeVoto's problems with narration may be related to Stegner's
own sense of developing mastery in the same area. It is certainly
true that the notion of ventriloquism has been one of his critical
touchstones for a long while, and that it helps to explain his high
esteem for Willa Cather. Indeed, it is no great stretch of the imagination to read Stegner's fine essay on *My Ántonia* as an exercise in
self-analysis and self-criticism.

Stegner argues that Willa Cather discovered her proper literary
"voice" when she began to write about the region and the people
she knew best. Then she wrote "spontaneously because she was
tapping both memory and affection."[5] We have said as much of
Wallace Stegner in our discussion of *The Big Rock Candy Mountain. My Ántonia,* he goes on, outstrips Cather's earlier novels in
the area of technique.

One technical device which is fundamental to the greater concentration and suggestiveness of *My Ántonia* is the point of view from which it is told. Both of the earlier "Nebraska novels" had been reported over the protagonist's shoulder, with omniscient intrusions by the author. Here the whole story is told by a narrator, Jim Burden, a boyhood friend of Ántonia, later a lawyer representing the railroads. The use of the narrative mask permits Miss Cather to exercise her sensibility without obvious self-indulgence: Burden becomes an instrument of the selectivity that she worked for.... Finally, Jim Burden is used constantly as a suggestive parallel to Ántonia.... In the process of understanding and commemorating Ántonia, he locates himself. (147)

Change the names and the passage amounts to a concise survey of Stegner's experiments with narrative point of view: in his early fiction Stegner was often awkwardly intrusive; then, with the advent of Joe Allston, came the discovery of a "narrative mask" that permitted him to exercise his own "sensibility without obvious self-indulgence" — to ventriloquize; finally, in Lyman Ward, Stegner developed an "instrument of the selectivity" he had long pursued, a narrator who "locates himself" in "the process of understanding and commemorating" his grandparents.

Similarities in characterization and theme are as remarkable as those of development and technique. The image of Ántonia — "A mine of life, the mother of races, a new thing forming itself in hardship and hope, but clinging to fragments of the well-loved old" (153) — embodies the essentials that turn up, their proportions modified, in Stegner's Elsa Mason, Marian Catlin, and Susan Burling Ward. Moreover, one of Cather's most recurrent questions — "how a frontier American may lift himself from his tradition-less, artless environment to full stature as an artist and an individual" (146) — is reopened in much of Stegner's major fiction. The similarity is far from coincidental, for in both writers we encounter a splendid unity of life and work. For Stegner, as for Cather, childhood experience on the remote frontier was at once a cultural obstacle and a tremendous cultural opportunity. While it loaded consciousness with personal images which would, upon inspection, flow into and blend with the larger patterns of regional and national life, the frontier did little to nourish the expressive skills essential to the making of art. Overcoming the obstacles necessarily involved leaving the frontier. Given time, determination, more than a little luck, and the mysterious compulsion to discipline memory with form, the imaginative return issued in important literature. The "cultural burden" that remains — a challenge as vital in *Angle of Repose* as it is in *The Big Rock Candy Mountain* — is to apply the knowledge of the past in molding the present and the future. No doubt Wallace Stegner will continue to carry this legacy that his mother bequeathed to him — the same "cultural burden that Willa Cather herself carried, the quintessentially American burden of remaking in terms of a new place everything that makes life graceful and civilized" (152).

Notes and References

Chapter One

1. Robin White and Ed McClanahan, "An Interview with Wallace Stegner," *Per/Se* 3 (Fall, 1968), 30.
2. Except where otherwise indicated, biographical materials have been selected from interviews with Wallace Stegner recorded on March 19 and March 20, 1973.
3. This exploit, modified somewhat, appears in *The Big Rock Candy Mountain* (New York, 1943), p. 10.
4. *Wolf Willow: A History, a Story and a Memory of the Last Plains Frontier* (New York, 1962), pp. 15–16. *Wolf Willow* is explicitly autobiographical in the presentation of materials which take fictionalized form in *The Big Rock Candy Mountain*. For a more detailed rendering of grandmother Stegner's decline, see "The Double Corner," in *The Women on the Wall* (New York, 1948), pp. 186–212.
5. *The Big Rock Candy Mountain,* p. 178.
6. White and McClanahan, p. 30.
7. *Wolf Willow,* p. 4. Hereafter the pagination of quotations from this volume is indicated in the text.
8. *The Big Rock Candy Mountain,* p. 403.
9. Ibid.
10. *Mormon Country* (New York, 1942), p. 62.
11. *The Big Rock Candy Mountain,* p. 506.
12. Phil Strong, *The Saturday Review of Literature* 16 (September 25, 1937), 5; review of *Remembering Laughter.*
13. Sinclair Lewis, "Fools, Liars, and Mr. DeVoto," *Saturday Review of Literature* 27 (April 15, 1944), 9.
14. Ibid., p. 11.

Chapter Two

1. *The Sound of Mountain Water* (Garden City, N.Y., 1969), p. 9. Hereafter the pagination of quotations from this volume is indicated in the text.
2. "A Democracy Built on Quicksand," *Delphian Quarterly* 22 (Autumn, 1939), 12. This essay is perhaps the best example of Stegner's early views on the Western predicament.

3. Sidney LaMarr Jenson takes this approach in his dissertation, "The Middle Ground: A Study of Wallace Stegner's Use of History in Fiction" (Ph.D. diss., University of Utah, 1972). Some of our arguments overlap Dr. Jenson's but were arrived at independently.

4. *Mormon Country,* p. 20. Hereafter the pagination of quotations from this volume is indicated in the text.

5. *The Gathering of Zion: The Story of the Mormon Trail* (New York, 1964), p. 314. Hereafter the pagination of quotations from this volume is indicated in the text.

6. *Beyond the Hundredth Meridian: John Wesley Powell and the Second Opening of the West* (Boston, 1954), vii. Hereafter the pagination of quotations from this volume is indicated in the text.

7. Joseph Henry Jackson, *San Francisco Chronicle,* "This World" section, September 12, 1954, p. 17; review of *Beyond the Hundredth Meridian.*

8. *Wolf Willow,* p. 96.

9. A suspenseful tale, "The Wolfer" was published separately in *Harper's Magazine* 219 (October, 1959), 53–61.

Chapter Three

1. Hemingway is suggesting that the writer must kill off his characters — physically or psychologically — in order to bring his work to a satisfying close. Stegner agrees with Hemingway but goes further. Like Chekhov and Forster, Stegner finds all fictional endings ultimately unsatisfying: "the book has to stop and the characters want to go on, and some violence has to be done to experience in order to give the piece of it incorporated into the story the air of finality." *Teaching the Short Story,* Davis Publications in English, No. 2 (Davis, Calif., 1965), pp. 3–4.

2. "The Making of Fiction," *Rocky Mountain Review* 6 (Fall, 1941), 3.

3. *Teaching the Short Story,* p. 4.

4. *The Writer in America* (Tokyo, n.d.), p. 96.

5. "The West Coast: Region with a View," *Saturday Review of Literature* 42 (May 2, 1959), 15.

6. *The Writer in America,* pp. 7–8.

7. "Is the Novel Done for?" *Harper's* 186 (December, 1942), 82.

8. "Variations on a Theme by Conrad," *Yale Review* 39 (1950), 513.

9. "Robert Frost: 'Lover's Quarrel with the World,'" *Stanford Today* 13 (March, 1961), unpaged.

10. Bernard DeVoto, *The Year of Decision: 1846* (Boston, 1943), unpaged.

11. *The Writer in America,* p. 3.

12. In 1952, Tokyo's Hokuseido Press published a third collection of Stegner stories, translated into Japanese by Mikio Hiramatsu. Intended

for a new readership, *The Blue-Winged Teal* deliberately excludes stories not collected in *The Women on the Wall* and in *The City of the Living.* Hence, separate consideration of this volume is unnecessary here.

13. "The Chink," in *The Women on the Wall* (Boston, 1950), p. 229. Hereafter the pagination of quotations from this volume is indicated in the text.

14. "The Blue-Winged Teal," *The City of the Living and Other Stories* (Boston, 1956), pp. 3, 7. Hereafter the pagination of quotations from this volume is indicated in the text.

15. "A Problem in Fiction" originally appeared in the *Pacific Spectator* 3 (1949), 368–75. It has since been republished in an unusual textbook which attempts to teach creative writing by example rather than precept, *The Writer's Art: A Collection of Short Stories,* ed. Wallace Stegner with Richard Scowcroft and Boris Ilyin (Boston, 1950), pp. 317–24.

Chapter Four

1. *Remembering Laughter* (Boston, 1937), p. 4. Hereafter the pagination of quotations from this volume is indicated in the text.

2. *On a Darkling Plain* (New York, 1940), p. 72. Hereafter the pagination of quotations from this volume is indicated in the text.

3. Archibald MacLeish, "Speech to those who say Comrade," in *Public Speech* (New York, 1936), unpaged.

4. See Catherine Drinker Bowen, "Bernard DeVoto: Historian, Critic, and Fighter," in Bernard DeVoto, *The Year of Decision: 1846* (Boston, 1961), p. xv.

5. *Fire and Ice* (New York, 1941), p. 3. Hereafter the pagination of quotations from this volume is indicated in the text.

6. Walter B. Rideout, *The Radical Novel in The United States, 1900–1954* (Cambridge, Mass., 1956), p. 286.

7. *The Big Rock Candy Mountain,* p. 438. Hereafter the pagination of quotations from this volume is indicated in the text.

8. Howard Mumford Jones, "World Out of Nowhere," *Saturday Review of Literature* 26 (October 2, 1943), 11; review of *The Big Rock Candy Mountain.*

9. Joseph Warren Beach, "Life-Size Stegner," *New York Times Book Review,* September 26, 1943, p. 4; review of *The Big Rock Candy Mountain.*

10. Edward Weeks, "Something for Nothing," *Atlantic* 172 (November, 1943), 128; review of *The Big Rock Candy Mountain.*

11. "Hostage," *Virginia Quarterly Review* 19 (Summer, 1943), 403–11, later collected in *The Women on the Wall,* pp. 146–56.

12. *Second Growth* (Boston, 1947), p. 82. Hereafter the pagination of quotations from this volume is indicated in the text.

13. We rely here on Gibbs M. Smith's compendious *Joe Hill* (Salt Lake City, 1969).

14. Ibid., p. 113.

15. "I Dreamed I Saw Joe Hill Last Night," *Pacific Spectator* 1 (Spring, 1947), 186.

16. "Joe Hill: The Wobblies' Troubadour," *New Republic* 118 (January 5, 1948), 20. Stegner's remarks on Joe Hill and the International Workers of the World did not go unanswered. See *New Republic* 118 (February 9, 1948), 38–39. *Time* reported (51 [April 19, 1948], 26) that IWW sympathizers picketed the *New Republic* office in protest over Stegner's "slur on their hero." Many historians of American labor would insist that the Wobblies were no more violent than the Pinkerton thugs and vigilantes who opposed them, and that Wobbly tactics were justified given the failure of political reform and the impoverished impotence of working men during the first decades of this century.

17. "Joe Hill: The Wobblies' Troubadour," p. 20.

18. Stegner reveals the extent of his research in a letter to the *New Republic* 118 (February 9, 1948), 38:

I have talked and corresponded with several dozen old-time Wobblies who were active in Joe Hill's time. Seven of them knew him personally; three of them knew him well.... I have photostatic copies of the only remaining volume of the trial transcript, plus complete files of the Deseret *News* and the Salt Lake *Tribune* from the time of Hill's arrest until his execution. I have the records of the Utah State Penitentiary, the statements of the Supreme Court and the Utah Pardon Board, the coverage of the case in the New York *Times* and various news magazines. I have checked the police records of San Pedro and Los Angeles and files of the Los Angeles papers, and I have consulted with the sheriff who executed Hill, jailers and law-enforcement officers who knew him, a member of his Defense Committee, the Swedish vice-consul who investigated the case for the Swedish Minister, the AP reporter who covered the case and witnessed the execution, the son of the man Joe Hill was supposed to have killed.

For excerpts from Stegner's correspondence concerning Joe Hill, see the text and notes in Smith, *Joe Hill*.

19. "Joe Hill: The Wobblies' Troubadour," p. 24.

20. *The Preacher and the Slave* (Boston, 1950), p. ix–x. Hereafter the pagination of quotations from this volume is indicated in the text. The novel was reissued as *Joe Hill* by Doubleday in 1969. Readers may wish to consult Stegner's comments on *The Preacher and the Slave* in *The Sound of Mountain Water,* pp. 206–7.

21. Gibbs M. Smith observes in *Joe Hill* (201): "Taking his cue from a letter Hill wrote to an unidentified preacher known only as Gus, Stegner created Gustave Lund, friend and confidant of Joe Hill."

Chapter Five

1. *A Shooting Star* (New York, 1961), p. 15. Hereafter the pagination of quotations from this volume is indicated in the text.
2. Paul Pickrel, "A Stegner, a MacLennan, and a Sontag," *Harper's* 224 (September, 1967), 118; review of *All the Little Live Things,* et al.
3. *All the Little Live Things* (New York, 1967), p. 54. Hereafter the pagination of quotations from this volume is indicated in the text.
4. Peter Buitenhuis, "Sunset Years in the West," *New York Times Book Review,* August 6, 1967, p. 30; review of *All the Little Live Things.*
5. We rely here on Rodman Paul's meticulous edition of Mary Hallock Foote's personal reminiscences, *A Victorian Gentlewoman in the Far West: The Reminiscences of Mary Hallock Foote* (San Marino, Calif., 1972). Hereafter the pagination of quotations from this volume is indicated in the text.
6. *Angle of Repose* (Garden City, N.Y., 1971), p. 441. Hereafter the pagination of quotations from this volume is indicated in the text.

Chapter Six

1. Garden City, New York, 1974, p. ix. Hereafter the pagination of quotations from this volume is indicated in the text.
2. Forrest G. Robinson and Margaret G. Robinson, "Wallace Stegner, an Interview," *Quarry* 4 (1974), 73.
3. Ibid.
4. Ibid.
5. "Willa Cather, *My Ántonia,*" in *The American Novel: From James Fenimore Cooper to William Faulkner,* ed., Wallace Stegner (New York, 1965), p. 145. Hereafter the pagination of quotations from this volume is indicated in the text.

Selected Bibliography

The record of nearly forty years of professional endeavor, this bibliography is necessarily selective. It cites first editions and American editions currently in print; other reprints and foreign editions are excluded. The lists of short fiction, articles, and essays are extensive but omit book reviews, encyclopedia entries, forewords, and introductions, as well as all items republished in monograph form.

PRIMARY SOURCES

1. Novels and Collected Short Fiction

Remembering Laughter. Boston: Little, Brown, 1937.
The Potter's House. Muscatine, Iowa: Prairie Press, 1938.
On a Darkling Plain. New York: Harcourt, Brace, 1940.
Fire and Ice. New York: Duell, Sloan, and Pearce, 1941.
The Big Rock Candy Mountain. New York: Duell, Sloan, and Pearce, 1943. Reprint. Garden City, N.Y.: Doubleday, 1973.
Second Growth. Boston: Houghton Mifflin, 1947.
The Preacher and the Slave. Boston: Houghton Mifflin, 1950. Reprinted as *Joe Hill: A Biographical Novel*. Garden City, N.Y.: Doubleday, 1969.
The Women on the Wall. Boston: Houghton Mifflin, 1950.
The Blue-Winged Teal. Translated into Japanese by Mikio Hiramatsu. Tokyo: Hokuseido Press, 1952.
The City of the Living, and Other Stories. Boston: Houghton Mifflin, 1956. Reprint. Plainview, N.J.: Books for Libraries, 1969.
A Shooting Star. New York: Viking, 1961.
All the Little Live Things. New York: Viking, 1967. Reprint. New York: New American Library, 1968.
Angle of Repose. Garden City, N.Y.: Doubleday, 1971. Reprint. New York: Fawcett World Library, 1972.
The Spectator Bird. Garden City, N.Y.: Doubleday, 1976.

2. Nonfiction in Monograph Form

Clarence Earl Dutton: An Appraisal. Salt Lake City, Utah: University of Utah, 1935.

Mormon Country. New York: Duell, Sloan, and Pearce, 1942. Reprint. New York: Hawthorn Books, 1975.

One Nation. With the editors of *Look.* Boston: Houghton Mifflin, 1945.

Look at America: The Central Northwest. With the editors of *Look.* Boston: Houghton Mifflin, 1947.

The Writer in America. Tokyo: Hokuseido Press, n.d. Reprint. Folcroft, Penn.: Folcroft Library Editions, 1951.

Beyond the Hundredth Meridian: John Wesley Powell and the Second Opening of the West. Boston: Houghton Mifflin, 1954. Reprint. Boston: Houghton Mifflin, 1962.

The Papers of Bernard DeVoto: A Description and a Checklist of His Work. San Francisco: Taylor and Taylor, 1960.

Wolf Willow: A History, a Story, and a Memory of the Last Plains Frontier. New York: Viking, 1962.

The Gathering of Zion: The Story of the Mormon Trail. New York: McGraw-Hill, 1964.

Teaching the Short Story. Davis Publications in English, No. 2. Davis, Calif.: University of California, 1965.

The Sound of Mountain Water. Garden City, N.Y.: Doubleday, 1969.

Discovery! The Search for Arabian Oil. Beirut: Middle East Export Press, 1971.

Variations on a Theme of Discontent. Logan, Utah: Utah State University Press, 1972.

Robert Frost and Bernard DeVoto. Stanford, Calif.: Associates of the Stanford University Libraries, 1974.

The Uneasy Chair: A Biography of Bernard DeVoto. Garden City, N.Y.: Doubleday, 1974.

3. Edited Works

An Exposition Workshop: Readings in Modern Controversy. Edited by Wallace Stegner, et al. Boston: Little, Brown, 1939.

Readings for Citizens at War. Edited by Wallace Stegner, et al. New York: Harper, 1941.

Stanford Short Stories, 1946. Edited by Wallace Stegner with Richard Scowcroft. Stanford, Calif.: Stanford University Press, 1947. (Subsequent volumes in this series are not cited in this bibliography.)

This Is Dinosaur, Echo Park, and Its Magic Rivers. Edited by Wallace Stegner. New York: Knopf, 1955.

Great American Short Stories. Edited by Wallace Stegner with Mary Stegner. New York: Dell, 1957.

POWELL, JOHN WESLEY. *The Exploration of the Colorado River of the West.* Edited by Wallace Stegner. Chicago: University of Chicago Press, 1957.

Selected American Prose, 1841-1900: The Realistic Movement. Edited by Wallace Stegner. New York: Rinehart, 1958. Reprint. Gloucester, Mass.: Peter Smith, 1963.

CLEMENS, SAMUEL. *The Adventures of Huckleberry Finn.* Edited by Wallace Stegner. New York: Dell, 1960.

HARTE, BRET. *The Outcasts of Poker Flat.* Edited by Wallace Stegner. New York: New American Library, 1961.

POWELL, JOHN WESLEY. *Report on the Lands of the Arid Regions of the United States: With a More Detailed Account of the Lands of Utah.* Edited by Wallace Stegner. Cambridge, Mass.: Harvard University Press, 1962.

The American Novel: From James Fenimore Cooper to William Faulkner. Edited by Wallace Stegner. New York: Basic Books, 1965.

GUTHRIE, A. B. *The Big Sky.* Edited by Wallace Stegner. Boston: Houghton Mifflin, 1965.

Twenty Years of Stanford Stories. Edited by Wallace Stegner, et al. Stanford, Calif.: Stanford University Press, 1966.

Effective Theme. Edited by Wallace Stegner, et al. New York: Holt, Rinehart, and Winston, 1967.

HAWTHORNE, NATHANIEL. *The Twice-Told Tales.* Edited by Wallace Stegner. New York: Heritage Press, 1967.

Modern Composition. Edited by Wallace Stegner, et al. Rev. ed. 6 vols. New York: Holt, Rinehart, and Winston, 1969.

The Writer's Art: A Collection of Short Stories. Edited by Wallace Stegner with Richard Scowcroft and Boris Ilyin. Boston: Heath, 1950. Reprint. Westport, Conn.: Greenwood Press, 1972.

DEVOTO, BERNARD. *The Letters of Bernard DeVoto.* Edited by Wallace Stegner. Garden City, N.Y.: Doubleday, 1975.

4. Uncollected Short Fiction

"Pete and Emil." *Salt Lake Tribune,* December 9, 1934, p. 3.

"Saskatchewan Idyll." *Monterey Beacon,* June 29, 1935, pp. 8–9.

"Home to Utah." *Story* 9 (August, 1936), 28–42.

"Bloodstain." *American Prefaces* 2 (Summer, 1937), 150–53.

"The Dam Builder." *Frontier and Midland* 17 (Summer, 1937), 231-36.

"Fish." *Intermountain Review* 1 (Summer, 1937) 1, 6–9.

"The Two Wives." *Redbook* 72 (July, 1938), 48–52, 65–66.

"The Noise Outside." *Redbook* 73 (January, 1939), 20–23, 70, 73.

"One Last Wilderness." *Scribner's* 105 (January, 1939), 16–20, 44–51, 60–65.

"One Thing at a Time." *Collier's* 106 (October 26, 1940), 20, 57–61.

"Say It with Flowers." *Mademoiselle* 12 (June, 1941), 60–61, 111–12, 115–16, 119, 122.

"The Four Mules of God." *Decision* 2 (October, 1941), 19–24.

"The Paradise Hunter." *Redbook* 82 (August, 1943), 24–30, 102–10; (September, 1943), 24–29, 99–108.

"House on Cherry Creek." *Collier's* 116 (August 11, 1945), 16–17.

"Admirable Crichton." *New Yorker* 22 (June 15, 1946), 52.

"He Who Spits at the Sky," *Esquire* 49 (March, 1958), 140–54.

"Something Spurious from the Mindanao Deep." *Harper's* 217 (August, 1958), 50–58.

"Indoor-Outdoor Living." *Pacifica* [Demonstration issue] (September, 1959), 16–23.

5. Uncollected Articles and Essays

"Can Teachers Be Writers?" *Intermountain Review* 1 (January 1, 1937), 1, 3.

"C. E. Dutton, Explorer, Geologist, Nature Writer." *Scientific Monthly* 45 (July, 1937), 83–85.

"What Is It?" *Writer* 50 (November, 1937), 342–44.

"The Trail of the Hawkeye." *Saturday Review of Literature* 18 (July 30, 1938), 3–4, 16–17.

"A Decade of Regional Publishing." *Publisher's Weekly* 135 (March 11, 1939), 1060–64.

"Publishing in the Provinces." *Delphian Quarterly* 22 (Summer, 1939), 2–7, 18.

"A Democracy Built on Quicksand." *Delphian Quarterly* 22 (Autumn, 1939), 11–15, 29.

"Regionalism in Art." *Delphian Quarterly* 22 (Winter, 1939), 2–7.

"'Truth' and 'Faking' in Fiction." *Writer* 53 (February, 1940), 40–43.

"Diagnosis and Prognosis." *Delphian Quarterly* 23 (Winter, 1940), 2–7, 55.

"Sword-Words and Words of Wisdom." *Delphian Quarterly* 24 (Summer, 1941), 2–5.

"The Tourist Revolution." *Delphian Quarterly* 24 (Summer, 1941), 34–38.

"Writer's Conference in the Rocky Mountains." *Providence Journal,* August 24, 1941, VI, p. 5.

"The Making of Fiction." *Rocky Mountain Review* 6 (Fall, 1941), 1, 3–4.

"Colleges in Wartime." *Delphian Quarterly* 25 (Spring, 1942), 2–7.

"Shaping of Experience." *Writer* 55 (April, 1942), 99–102.

"The Little Man with the Purchasing Power." *Delphian Quarterly* 25 (Summer, 1942), 9–15.

"The Naturalization of an Idea." *Delphian Quarterly* 25 (Autumn, 1942), 31–36, 43.

"Is the Novel Done For?" *Harper's* 186 (December, 1942), 76–83.

"The Co-operatives and the Peace." *Delphian Quarterly* 26 (Spring, 1943), 15–18.

"The Turtle at Home." *Atlantic* 171 (April, 1943), 123, 127.

"The Co-ops in Crisis." *Delphian Quarterly* 26 (Winter, 1943), 15–18, 50.

"Get Out of That Story!" *Writer* 56 (December, 1943), 360–62.

"Who Persecutes Boston?" *Atlantic* 174 (July, 1944), 45–52.

"We Reach for the Sky." *Mademoiselle* 15 (September, 1944), 55–56, 108–14.

"Crown Thy Good with Brotherhood." *Delphian Quarterly* 27 (Winter, 1944), 18–22.

"In America You Say It with Flowers." *Common Ground* 5 (Summer, 1945), 76–80.

"The Nisei Come Home." *New Republic* 113 (July 9, 1945), 45–46.

"They Came to Pick Crops." *Ammunition* 8 (August, 1945), 10–11.

"Jews Are the Most Misunderstood Minority." *Glamour* 12 (July, 1946), 75–78.

"Education for Democracy — the Victory of Portola Heights." *Reader's Scope* 4 (September, 1946), 87 89.

"I Dreamed I Saw Joe Hill Last Night." *Pacific Spectator* 1 (Spring, 1947), 184–87.

"400 Families Plan a House." *'47* 1 (April, 1947), 63–67.

"The Fretful Porcupine." *'47* 1 (May, 1947), 87–91.

"Pattern for Demagogues." *Pacific Spectator* 2 (1948), 399–411.

"Joe Hill: The Wobblies' Troubadour." *New Republic* 118 (January 5, 1948), 20–24, 38.

"Correspondence: Joe Hill." *New Republic* 118 (February 9, 1948), 38–39.

"New Climates for the Writer." *New York Times Book Review,* March 7, 1948, pp. 1, 20.

"Meeting Crisis with Understanding; UNESCO." *Pacific Spectator* 2 (Summer, 1948), 241–52.

"The Anxious Generation." *English Journal* 10 (January, 1949), 183–88.

"Jack Sumner and John Wesley Powell." *Colorado Magazine* 26 (January, 1949), 61–69.

"A Problem in Fiction." *Pacific Spectator* 3 (Fall, 1949), 368–75.

"Writing as Graduate Study." *College English* 2 (1950), 429–32.

"Hometown Revisited: 15. Salt Lake City." *Tomorrow* 9 (February, 1950), 26–29.

"The Teaching and Studying of Writing (A Symposium)." *Western Review* 14 (Spring, 1950), 165–79.

"Variations on a Theme by Conrad." *Yale Review* 39 (March, 1950), 512–23.

"Why I Like the West." *Tomorrow* 9 (July, 1950), 5–9.

"Backroads of the American West." *Tomorrow* 10 (October, 1950), 9–14.

"Literary Lessons Out of Asia." *Pacific Spectator* 5 (1951), 413–19.

"India: Crowds, Resignation, and the Cominform Line." *Reporter* 4 (February 20, 1951), 6–10.

"Renaissance in Many Tongues." *Saturday Review of Literature* 34 (August 4, 1951), 27-28, 52-54.

"The Timid Ambassador." *Reporter* 5 (September 4, 1951), 33-35.

"Cairo, 1950." *Pacific Spectator* 5 (Winter, 1951), 42-47.

"Everything Potent Is Dangerous." In *This I Believe,* compiled by Edward R. Murrow, pp. 173-74. New York: Simon and Schuster, 1952.

"One-fourth of a Nation: Public Lands and Itching Fingers." *Reporter* 8 (May 12, 1953), 25-29.

"Battle for the Wilderness." *New Republic* 130 (February 15, 1954), 13-15.

"What Besides Talent?" *Author and Journalist* 41 (March, 1956), 11-13, 29.

"America's Mightiest Playground." *Holiday* 20 (July, 1956), 35-42, 122-25.

"Twenty Years of *Western Review:* A Series of Recollections." *Western Review* 20 (Winter, 1956), 87-89.

"The World's Strangest Sea." *Holiday* 21 (May, 1957), 76-77, 176-85.

"The Rocky Mountain West." In *The Romance of North America,* edited by H. Mosley, pp. 363-92. Boston: Houghton Mifflin, 1958.

"Love Affair with the Heber Valley, U.S.A." *Vogue* 131 (February 1, 1958), 132-33, 192-93.

"One Way to Spell Man." *Saturday Review of Literature* 41 (May 24, 1958), 8-11, 43-44.

"California's Gold Rush Country." *Holiday* 24 (August, 1958), 64-69, 127.

"The American Student, A Teacher's View." *Saturday Review of Literature* 41 (September 13, 1958), 23.

"Sensibility and Intelligence." *Saturday Review of Literature* 41 (December 13, 1958), 24.

"The War between the Rough Riders and the Bird Watchers." *Sierra Club Bulletin* 44 (May, 1959), 4-11.

"The West Coast: Region with a View." *Saturday Review of Literature* 42 (May 2, 1959), 15-17, 41.

"To a Young Writer." *Atlantic* 204 (November, 1959), 88-91.

"Celebrated Jumping Freud." *Reporter* 22 (March 17, 1960), 45-46.

"Robert Frost: 'A Lover's Quarrel with the World.'" *Stanford Today* 13 (March, 1961), unpaged.

"Our Saddest War." *Coronet* 49 (April, 1961), 62-81.

"Corsica Out of Season." *Harper's* 223 (October, 1961), 75-79.

"A Dedication to the Memory of John Wesley Powell." *Arizona and the West* 4 (Spring, 1962), 1-4.

"To an Anonymous Admirer." *Sequoia* 7 (Spring, 1962), 1-7.

"Megalopolis and the Country All Around." *Living Wilderness* 82 (Winter, 1962), 23-24.

"The Great Mountains." *American Heritage Book of Great Natural Wonders,* edited by Alvin V. Josephy, pp. 209–303. New York: American Heritage, 1963.

"The Personality." In *Four Portraits and One Subject: Bernard DeVoto,* pp. 79-108. Boston: Houghton Mifflin, 1963.

"Western Record and Romance." In *Literary History of the United States,* edited by R. E. Spiller, et al., 3rd ed. rev., pp. 862–77. New York: Macmillan, 1963.

"Creative Writer as an Image Maker." *Writer* 76 (October, 1963), 24.

"Patterns of Alienation." *Fullbright Review* 1 (Fall, 1964), 3–10.

"Quiet Crisis or Lost Cause." *Saturday Review of Literature* 47 (September 19, 1964), 28, 50.

"Theodore Dreiser." In *American Literary Masters,* edited by C. R. Anderson, et al., vol. 2, pp. 631–41. New York: Holt, Rinehart, and Winston, 1965.

"Thomas Wolfe." In *American Literary Masters,* edited by C. R. Anderson, et al., vol. 2, pp. 1071–81. New York: Holt, Rinehart, and Winston, 1965.

"Goodbye to All T——t!" *Atlantic* 215 (March, 1965), 119.

"What Ever Happened to the Great Outdoors?" *Saturday Review of Literature* 48 (May 22, 1965), 37–38.

"Myths of the Western Dam." *Saturday Review of Literature* 48 (October 23, 1965), 29–31.

"To Save the Grand Canyon." *Saturday Review of Literature* 49 (August 20, 1966), 20.

"The People against the American Continent." *Vermont History* 35 (1967), 177–85.

"Legislating to Save the Land." *Saturday Review of Literature* 50 (January 14, 1967), 90–92.

"Last Chance for the Everglades." *Saturday Review of Literature* 50 (May 6, 1967), 22–23, 72–73.

"On Censorship." *Arts in Society* 4 (Summer, 1967), 281–99.

"Class of '67: The Gentle Desperadoes." *Nation* 204 (June 19, 1967), 480–81.

"Hard Experience Talking." *Saturday Review of Literature* 50 (August 19, 1967), 25.

"California: The Experimental Society." *Saturday Review of Literature* 50 (September 23, 1967), 28.

"Professor O'Connor at Stanford." In *Michael/Frank: Studies on Frank O'Connor,* edited by Maurice Sheehy, pp. 94-102. New York: Knopf, 1969.

"Lake Powell." *Holiday* 39 (May, 1969), 64–69.

"Conservation Equals Survival." *American Heritage* 21 (December, 1969), 12–15.

"Re-discovery: Wescott's *Goodbye Wisconsin.*" *Southern Review* 6 (1970), 674–81.

"East Palo Alto." *Saturday Review of Literature* 53 (August 1, 1970), 12, 15, 54.

"Last Exit to America." *Esquire* 77 (April, 1972), 87–89, 168–70, 175.

"Thoughts in a Dry Land." *Westways* 64 (September, 1972), 14–19, 58.

"Walter Clark's Frontier." *Atlantic* 232 (August, 1973), 94–98.

"Oregon Coast." *Travel and Leisure* 2 (Autumn, 1973), 42–43, 80–81.

"This New Man, the American." *Stanford Magazine* 1 (Fall/Winter, 1973), 14–19.

"Letter from Canada." *American West* 11 (January, 1974), 28–30.

"The Great Amazonian Plain." *Travel and Leisure* 4 (February, 1974), 31, 47–49.

"The Provincial Consciousness." *University of Toronto Quarterly* 43 (Summer, 1974), 299–310.

"I Sing of America." *Holiday* 56 (March, 1975), 36, 49.

"Depression Pop." *Esquire* 84 (September, 1975), 79–83, 154.

SECONDARY SOURCES

ABRAHAMS, WILLIAM. "The Real Thing." *Atlantic* 227 (April, 1971), 96–97. Review of *Angle of Repose.*

BURKE, HATTAN. "The Ninth Circle: Three Novels." *Sewanee Review* 70 (Winter, 1962), 169–76. Brief analysis of Stegner's *A Shooting Star* and two other contemporary novels as examples of "the search for identity in a world despiritualized, mechanized, and deterministic."

CANZONERI, ROBERT. "Wallace Stegner: Trial by Existence." *Southern Review* 9 (1973), 796–827. Well documented tribute to Stegner's special brand of humanistic realism.

CLAYTON, JAMES L. "From Pioneers to Provincials: Mormonism as Seen by Wallace Stegner." *Dialogue: A Journal of Mormon Thought* 1 (Winter, 1966), 105–14. Review of *Mormon Country* and *The Gathering of Zion* which argues that Stegner's "non-religious humanism" produces a sympathetic rendering of Mormon pioneers but prevents the development of "a sustained chord of respect for the Mormon religion in the present age."

COWLEY, MALCOLM. "The Failed Novelist and the Successful Critic." *New York Times Book Review,* February 10, 1974, pp. 1–2. Review of *The Uneasy Chair: A Biography of Bernard DeVoto.*

EISINGER, CHESTER E. "Twenty Years of Wallace Stegner." *College English* 20 (1958), 110–16. Midcareer assessment of Stegner as a "representative" contemporary writer who has rejected radical social and political alternatives and turned to the exploration of self.

————. "Wallace Stegner: The Uncommitted." In *Fiction of the Forties,* pp. 324–28. Chicago: University of Chicago Press, 1963. Condensation of the preceding article set in the context of the "existential crisis" of the 1940s.

FLORA, JOSEPH M. "Vardis Fisher and Wallace Stegner: Teacher and Student." *Western American Literature* 5 (Summer, 1970), 122–28. Analyzes Fisher's influence on Stegner's work — most notably, the novelette *Remembering Laughter* and the short story, "The View from the Balcony."

HAIRSTON, JOE B. "The Westerner's Dilemma." Ph.D. dissertation, University of Minnesota, 1971. Hairston argues that Stegner, A. B. Guthrie, and Walter Van Tilburg Clark share a common faith in "the great community" antithetical to the stereotypical Western belief in self-sufficiency and rootless individualism.

HUDSON, LOIS PHILLIPS. "*The Big Rock Candy Mountain:* No Roots — and No Frontier." *South Dakota Review* 9 (Spring, 1971), 3–13. Assesses Stegner's achievement in light of the special dilemma of the Western writer, who is "charged with the double burden of dispelling myth and then building fiction on the fact they must first insist upon."

JENSON, SIDNEY L. "The Compassionate Seer: Wallace Stegner's Literary Artist." *Brigham Young University Studies* 14 (Winter, 1974), 248–62. Compendium of Stegner's views on the literary enterprise — its larger objectives and specific techniques.

————. "The Middle Ground: A Study of Wallace Stegner's Use of History in Fiction." Ph.D. dissertation, University of Utah, 1972. Meticulously detailed examination of Stegner's work in the context of "the middle ground."

LEWIS, MERRILL, and LEWIS, LORENE. *Wallace Stegner.* Boise State College Western Writers Series, No. 4. Boise: Boise State College, 1972. Useful forty-page pamphlet, providing a concise but comprehensive survey of the Stegner canon.

MILTON, JOHN. "Conversation with Wallace Stegner." *South Dakota Review* 9 (Spring, 1971), 45–57. Stegner discusses the special challenges faced by the Western writer.

MOSLEY, RICHARD. "First-Person Narration in Wallace Stegner's *All the Little Live Things.*" *Notes on Contemporary Literature* 3 (March, 1973), 12–13. Detailed examination of one of Stegner's most successful literary devices — the first person narrator.

PETERSON, AUDREY C. "Narrative Voice in Stegner's *Angle of Repose.*" *Western American Literature* 10 (Summer, 1975), 125–33. Defines Lyman Ward's complex narrative role and defends it as one "exactly suited to the need for a confrontation between the values of the past and those of today."

ROBINSON, FORREST G., and ROBINSON, MARGARET G. "Wallace Stegner: An Interview." *Quarry* 4 (1975), 72–84. Stegner discusses cultural and generational conflict, both within his own work and within the larger context of the American West.

SAPORTA, MARC. "Wallace Stegner." *Informations et documents* 187 (September 15–October 1, 1963), 23–26. Brief, French-language interview.

TYLER, ROBERT L. "The I.W.W. and the West." *American Quarterly* 12 (Summer, 1960), 175–87. Traces the myth of the I.W.W. "from an organization of dangerous, foreign 'syndicalists,' . . . to a jolly band of rogues ushering out the last frontier." Comment on the use of this myth by Stegner and other American writers.

WHITE, ROBIN, and McCLANAHAN, ED. "An Interview with Wallace Stegner." *Per Se* 3 (Fall, 1968), 28–35. Emphasizes biographical information and Stegner's views on the generation gap. Includes commentary by former students in the Stanford Creative Writing Program.

WILLEY, JILL LUCAS. "Wallace Stegner: An Annotated Bibligoraphy." M.A. dissertation, California State University, San Jose, 1975. Covers the following categories of Stegner's work: "Books — Fiction," "Books — Non-Fiction," "Story Collections and Single Stories," "Editions and Texts," "Articles and Essays," "Introductions and Contributions," "Book Reviews." Annotations and lists of critical reviews are provided when appropriate.

Index

185